LIVERPOOL

an ALTERNATIVE GUIDE

Bel Shaw

Additional photos by Jonathan Wyn

Blue Moon Publishing

First published in 2012 by: Blue Moon Publishing, Epsom KT17 9LD

The contents of this publication are correct at the time of printing, but may be subject to change as Liverpool continues to to be developed.

Printed by Argent Litho Limited

ISBN 978-0-9573563-0-6

Dedicated to Dad and Jamie

ACKNOWLEDGEMENTS

A Huge Thanks to Brian, Neil & Keith for all their expertise, – Jeanie for proof reading,
to Barry for his patience; most of the time! – Linda and Pattie for their support,
to jono for his photo contributions and for his company as we walked the streets
in all kinds of weather, and to all who helped to keep my spirits up
as I wrote this guide book.

INTRODUCTION

This book is an informal guide to the some of Liverpool's many statues, sculptures and buildings. A collection of facts and anecdotes about some of the familiar figures and structures, ranging from the great and good of the Industrial and Commercial time through to the more modern and controversial pieces.

Statues that are so familiar but over time have lost their relevance. Those statues that we pass by and are to the most part a mystery to us. Who were these illustrious figures and what had they contributed to Liverpool to justify a place on a plinth?

With the aid of photographs and illustrations, I hope to put flesh back on the bones of these figures and present them in a more human light, warts and all but at the same time to recognise their achievements and contribution to the growth and pride in Liverpool that we still feel today.

As Liverpool is a walkable city, I have broken the guide book up into districts, each with its own distinctive style and with the aid of maps to make it easier to pick out the statues and places of interest.

Enjoy the city and I hope this guide will be both informative and entertaining, to both the tourist and fellow Liverpudlians.

A Brief History

The meaning of the word ``Liverpool'' is open to debate. Originally known as Liuerpul, meaning a pool of muddy water, possibly derived from the Welsh words Llif, meaning a flood, and pwll meaning a pool or inlet.

Liverpool was little more than a fishing hamlet until 1207 when King John granted it the status of an official town in his Royal Charter. He recognised it as a prime site for mooring his ships and sending troops to the newly conquered Ireland. Tax concessions and land was also granted to anybody who settled there and its location as a port led to a steady growth both in trade and in the population.

One of its earliest sites was Liverpool Castle, built around 1235, the site of which is now occupied by the Victoria Monument in Derby Square.

The original street plan of Liverpool was believed to have been laid out by King John, the seven main streets took on the shape of the letter H, these streets were:

Castle Street
Chapel Street
Dale Street
Boncke (now Water Street)
Juggler Street (now High Street)
Moor Street (now Tithebarn Street)
Whiteacre Street (now Old Hall Street)

It is claimed that Liverpool is built on seven hills, which are recognised as the following:

Walton Hill

Everton Ridge/Brow

High Park/Toxteth Ridge

Mossley Hill

Allerton Hill

Olive Mount

Woolton Ridge/Camp Hill

The original port of Liverpool was situated where Liverpool One now stands. This pool became the site of what was to become the first commercial enclosed dock in the world, built in 1715 and with a capacity to hold one hundred ships. The remains of the dock wall can be seen through a viewing area within the Liverpool One car park.

By the 18th Century Liverpool's population had grown from 5,000 to 78,000 built mainly on the back of its involvement with the slave trade. Goods manufactured in Britain were sent via Liverpool to West Africa and exchanged for slaves who were then transported to the Americas and those ships returned to Liverpool laden with tobacco, sugar and cotton which had been produced by slave labour.

This profitable trade brought merchants and great wealth to the city and Liverpool enjoyed a boom time with many public buildings being erected, financed by local philanthropists, many of whom had made their fortune by direct or indirect association with the slave trade. At one time ten out of fourteen large banks in Liverpool were owned by slave traders and between 1787 and 1807 every Mayor of Liverpool had close connections with this trade.

After the abolition of slavery in 1807 Liverpool still had a very strong trade in cotton, supplying the Lancashire mills via the Manchester ship canal and from the 1830's with rail links.

By the end of the 19th Century, 40% of the world's trade passed through the port. The population grew quickly especially in the 1840's as a result of the Irish potato famine when many Irish families were forced to leave Ireland to make a new life, many of them moving to Liverpool.

By the 20th Century Liverpool took a downward turn. Faced with strong competition from abroad, traditional manufacturing industries suffered a sharp decline. Together with the introduction of shipping containers the once thriving docks became obsolete and Liverpool's economy suffered greatly.

Nowadays however, Liverpool has seen a resurgence and regeneration is having a beneficial effect within the city.

Liverpool is once more a thriving city, rich with a diverse cultural heritage making it a city with many attractions to cater for many tastes.

Georgian Quarter

Bordered by the Metropolitan Cathedral to the north and the Anglican Cathedral to the south, the Georgian Quarter sits on a hill, looking down on the city. Once the home of wealthy merchants wanting to escape the bustle of the city, the area is set out in a grid pattern of Georgian style houses. In fact there are more Georgian buildings in Liverpool than Bath. This area is recognised as the artistic, bohemian district and the majority of university buildings are within this area.

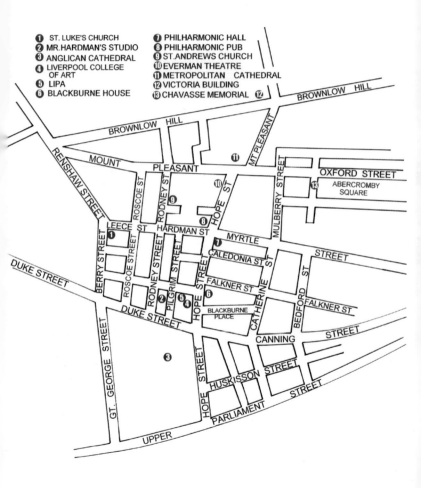

① ST. LUKE'S CHURCH
② MR. HARDMAN'S STUDIO
③ ANGLICAN CATHEDRAL
④ LIVERPOOL COLLEGE OF ART
⑤ LIPA
⑥ BLACKBURNE HOUSE
⑦ PHILHARMONIC HALL
⑧ PHILHARMONIC PUB
⑨ ST. ANDREWS CHURCH
⑩ EVERMAN THEATRE
⑪ METROPOLITAN CATHEDRAL
⑫ VICTORIA BUILDING
⑬ CHAVASSE MEMORIAL

As the result of a national competition Giles Gilbert Scott, a twenty two year old student architect was chosen to design the Anglican cathedral. However due to Scott's inexperience, the Cathedral committe appointed architect George F.Bodley to oversee the design and building work. This appointment was later to cause much friction between the two men who both had conflicting views as to the design and construction. Such was the anomosity between them that Scott was on the verge of resigning when Bodley unexpectedly fell ill and in 1907 died. This gave the freedom that Scott needed. Unhappy with his original twin tower design he went back to the Cathedral committee and after much persuasion by him, they accepted his new drawing. Instead of his original drawing of twin towers Scott replaced them with one massive central tower, and so work went ahead following the new plans.

The foundation stone was laid in 1904 by King Edward VII but the building was not completed until 1978. The first part of the Cathedral to be consecrated was the Lady Chapel in 1910. This part of the Cathedral was dedicated by Cosmo Lang, Archbishop of York and Bishop Chavasse, the father of Noel Chavasse who was later to become captain in the Medical Corps of the King's Regiment during World War I and to be awarded the V.C. twice.

Within the Lady Chapel are two stained glass windows depicting "Noble Women" from different walks of life who had made a contribution to the community both locally and nationaly. Local women, Kitty Wilkinson, helper of the poor and Agnes Jones, devoted nurse are included in the windows.

Carved into the walls of the Lady Chapel is a verse from St.John's Gospel (ch3:16).

"For God so loved the world that he gave his only begotten son, that whosoever believeth in him should not perish, but have everlasting life"

The massive central tower or Vestey Tower, so named after the benefactor, is 101metres high; access to the top and exterior of the tower is by way of two lifts and 108 steps. On a clear day there are spectacular views reaching as far as the Welsh Hills to the west, the Penines to the east and Blackpool Tower to the north.

The Vestey Tower also houses a set of bells which are not only the highest in the world but they also have the heaviest peal. Called the Bartlett Bells after Thomas Bartlett, a native of Liverpool who bequeathed the funding. There are thirteen bells in total, the Great George, named after George V is the heaviest weighing fourteen and a half tons. Too heavy to be swung, it hangs in one position and is struck with a hammer. Each bell has an

inscription taken from the Old and New Testament and each one has a name; the fourth, Gilbert is named after Giles Gilbert Scott. There are also initials on each bell which spelling out the name of Thomas Bartlett, whose ashes are housed in the ringing room.

On the floor of the main aisle is a circular design made from marble,the circle represents the base outline of the Great George and within it is an inscription commemorating Sir Giles work.

The Anglican Cathedral is also the only Cathedral to have a red telephone box, (not connected!) installed within the interior, a tribute to Sir Gilbert Scott as he was responsible for the design of this iconic telephone box. Sir Giles also went on to design Bankside Power Station in London, a massive generating station itself on the grand scale of a cathedral. Over time the power station fell into disuse but it was later redeveloped and in 2000 the building opened as the Tate Modern Art Gallery.

The building of the Cathedral lasted the rest of Scott's life. He never saw it completed as he died in 1960.Although he was a Roman Catholic, Scott is buried with his wife, outside the west porch of the Cathedral.

St James Cemetery

Beneath the shadow of the Anglican Cathedral is St. James cemetery. This area was once a quarry which provided sandstone for the ever growing town. When the quarry was exhausted a cemetery was created, designed by John Foster, a local architect. Within the grounds many illustrious city people were interred. During the nineteen thirties the cemetery fell into disuse and the area became a place to avoid. However this once neglected and overgrown cemetery has been transformed into a sunken garden with many of the tombs being placed against the sandstone walls that enclose the cemetery.

There are three connecting tunnels to the cemetery. The first tunnel, lined with gravestones, is also an entrance to the grounds and carved into the sandstone walls are the initials of stonemasons who worked there. At the bottom of the path and to the left, is a bricked up tunnel entrance which was used to transport heavy materials out of the quarry. To the right of this tunnel, if you look carefully, you will be able to pick out graffiti which had been scratched into the sandstone by 18th century navvies who were employed to excavate the tunnels.

The third tunnel which is also bricked up was used for funeral processions. It is believed that access was gained via the junction of Rodney Street, St. James Street and Duke Street.

Against the wall below the Cathedral are gravestones of children from the orphan asylums, each gravestone has row upon row of names of the boys and girls. Another grave shows the names of pupils from the Bluecoat Hospital School.

Flowing from the east wall is a natural spring or chalybeate (mineral) spring. It was discovered by a quarry worker at around 1773, and is said to have curative properties. The spring water is apparently safe to drink; I have tried it with no ill effects!

An inscription is still visible which says:

``*Christian reader view in me an emblem of true charity, who freely what I have bestow.Though neither heard nor seen to flow And I have full returns from Heaven for every cup of water given.*''

John Foster 1787-1846

Liverpool born son of John Foster Snr, an architect and surveyor to the Corporation of Liverpool, he followed in his father's footsteps by also making his career as an architect.

Amongst many of his local achievements was his design for St. James cemetery.

Foster was also responsible for the Oratory, which is situated at the entrance to the cemetery, nos. 2-10 Gambier Terrace, St Lukes (the bombed out church) and St Andrews church in Rodney Street are all accredited to Foster.

John Foster is suitably buried in St James cemetery immediately behind William Huskisson's mausoleum; and there is also an inscription to him in the Oratory which reads:

``On his return from long and arduous travels in the pursuit of his art, he enriched his native town with the fruits of his genius, industry and integrity.''

William Huskisson 1770-1830

The most striking monument in the cemetery is that belonging to Liverpool M.P. William Huskisson.

William Huskisson entered the cabinet in 1822 when he was appointed President of the Board of Trade and in the following year he was elected as M.P. for Liverpool. Huskisson worked closely with the merchants of the city and became a strong representative of their commercial interests. He played a major role in reducing import duties for sugar, cotton, and paper amongst other goods, all of which were being imported into the ever expanding warehouses along the waterfront.

When Wellington became Prime Minister in 1828, Huskisson refused to serve under him and so resigned his post. As a result Huskisson was able to give more of his time to various reforms.

He was keen supporter of the developing rail system, and in 1830 as M.P. for Liverpool, Huskisson was invited by the directors of the Liverpool and Manchester Railway to attend the opening of the new branch line connecting Liverpool to Manchester. The event drew an enormous crowd who had come to see the trains, especially Stephenson's new locomotive, The Rocket which was making its debut.

After cutting the ribbon and declaring the line open Huskisson then rode down the line with various other dignitaries amongst whom was the Duke of Wellington. Their train was pulled by the Northumbrian driven by George Stephenson. As the train stopped to take on water the party stepped down from the carriage onto the track to stretch their legs only to be surprised by the sound of the approaching Rocket which was travelling at some speed. Struggling to climb back into the carriage Huskisson lost his balance and he fell back onto the rails in front of the approaching engine. Huskisson was struck, his legs being badly injured and despite being rushed to the local hospital he died later that day. His dying words were:

``*I have met my death*''

On hearing of Huskisson's fate, Wellington, who was not an admirer, was heard to remark that the accident had been "a true act of God"

Huskisson was laid to rest in St James cemetery in the imposing mausoleum complete with a marble statue of his likeness .The statue remained in the mausoleum until 1968 when it was moved to the Walker Art Gallery as it was showing signs of wear. Huskisson's wife Emily commissioned a second statue for the Custom House in Liverpool and this now stands in the grounds of Pimlico Gardens, London having been moved there when the Custom House was demolished.

There is a dock named after him and in the Georgian quarter a street takes his name.

Sir William Brown. 1784-1864

Born in County Antrim, the eldest son of a Belfast linen merchant. In 1800 the family moved to Baltimore, America where William joined his father in the family business of Alex Brown and Sons which went on to become one of the leading investment banks in America in the nineteenth century. Moving to Liverpool in 1809 to run the English branch of the business Brown eventually moved out of linen and cotton trading into merchant banking, setting up his own bank and amassing a fortune handling the finances of the Liverpool merchants.

William Brown was also a prominent figure becoming involved in the political scene of Liverpool, he was elected M.P. for South Lancashire in 1826.He promoted the reform of the Liverpool Docks and in 1831 helped to establish the Bank of Liverpool. For his contribution to the city William Brown was made Freeman of the City.

His most lasting contribution to Liverpool was to donate £40,000, the cost of establishing a library. The William Brown Library was opened in 1860 and the street was renamed William Brown Street in his honour.

In 1862 William Brown was made Baronet in recognition of his "eminent commercial position and generous conduct towards the public of Liverpool."

William Brown died in 1884, his vault is built into the east wall of the cemetery below Hope Street.

Edward Rushton 1756-1814

Born in Liverpool Edward Rushton was apprenticed at the age of eleven to the East Indian Shipping Company of Watt and Gregson. He rose quickly through the ranks to become second mate on a slave ship. Having witnessed the brutal treatment of the slaves on board ship, Rushton's outspoken views led to him being charged with mutiny. Sadly during this journey he developed an eye infection which led to blindness. Returning home and being unsuitable for life as a mariner Rushton spent several years in a state of poverty. His views on the slave trade did not diminish however and during the 1780's he began an association with other like-minded Liverpool men, namely William Roscoe, Dr.Currie, William Shepherd and William Rathbone. With Roscoe, Dr.Currie and Rathbone, Edward Rushton went on to establish an institute for the blind. A purpose built school, designed by John Foster was opened in London Road in 1800.

Following an operation in 1807 Rushton's eyesight was restored enabling him to see his wife and children for the first time.

Edward Rushton died in November 1814 and his grave can be found within the grounds of St. James cemetery.

Edward Rushton died in November 1814 and his grave can be foundwithin the grounds of St. James cemetery.

Robert Cain 1826-1907

Born in County Cork, Ireland, Robert Cain's family moved to Liverpool when he was a boy. After a time at sea as a merchant sailor Robert Cain returned to his adopted city and set himself up as a publican and brewer. The venture proved so profitable that he was able to aquire a number of public houses, at one time he owned over two hundred pubs on Merseyside, three notable ones which are still operating are the highly ornate "Vines ," (Big House) "Central" and "Philharmonic"

Robert Cain was made a Lord with the title, Lord Brocket and as his business grew, he bought out Hindley's Brewery and moved into the purpose built premises in Stanhope Street, where Cain's Brewery stands to this day.

During his time as a brewer Robert Cain amassed a fortune, a popular figure in Liverpool, on his death in 1907, over 3,000 mourners attended his funeral.

Captain Elisha Lindsey Halsey

There are several gravestones with a nautical reference and one fascinating gravestone belongs to Captain Elisha Lindsey Halsey who came to an "untimely death" on board his ship the Thomas Bennett in the Bay of Biscay. During a fight on board ship he was stabbed to death by the ship's cook, Liverpool born John Kent. Kent stood trial for murder in Liverpool but was aquitted after pleading self defence

William Daniels (1813-1844)

Known as the Rembrandt of Liverpool, William Daniels was born and raised in Scotland Road. The son of a brickmaker he began work in his father's business at a very young age. He showed a talent for moulding the clay into figures and this came to the attention of a neighbour Mr. Mosses, a wood engraver who also happened to be a lecturer at the Royal Institution Liverpool. Mosses persuaded Daniel's father to send his son to the college for lessons in drawing. William attended classes and he soon won first prize for figure drawing.Daniels became apprenticed to Mosses as a wood engraver and in the evenings he worked on developing his painting skills.At the age of seventeen Daniels was invited to exhibit at the Liverpool Academy Exhibition. William began to take on commissions for portrait painting,gaining commissions from the local merchants, amongst them the brewer Robert Cain and corn broker, politician Sir Joshua Walmsley. Although Sir Joshua Walmsley became his patron William did not fully achieve his potential as a painter. He died aged thirty one, drink and his lifestyle having affected his health.The Walker Art Gallery has three examples of his work on show.

Captain John Oliver (1774-1876

John Oliver was born in Tavistock, Devon in 1774. At the age of ten he ran away from home to join the navy. He served his apprenticeship and became a seaman in 1794. Press ganged twice his life at sea saw him fighting at the Battle of the Nile, Copenhagen and serving on Nelson's ship, the Victory at the Battle of Trafalgar. After the war he found his way to Liverpool where he served in the Merchant Navy becoming master of several ships and only retiring at the age of eighty five. John Oliver went to live with his son in Toxteth, where he lived to the grand age of 102. He died on 27th March 1876 and his funeral at St. James Cemetery was attended by over one hundred people. Seamen from H.M.S. Eagle were pallbearers, with his coffin draped in the Union Flag. 1907, over 3,000 mourners attended his funeral.

William Hanson (1813-1860)

First Captain of the Great Eastern, Isambard Kingdom Brunel's great iron built ship, the mast of which stands outside the Kop at Liverpool Football Stadium. The link to Liverpool and Brunel's Great Eastern? Brunel's ships were based in Liverpool.The Great Eastern was finally broken up in 1889-1890 and the top mast bought by Liverpool Football Club for the team flag.

Sarah Biffen 1784-1850

Sarah Biffen was born In Somerset into a farming family. Sarah was born without arms and with underdeveloped legs, she only grew to the height of 94cm (37") tall. As a young girl Sarah was making a living as an exhibit in a travelling show and being looked after by a Mr.Dukes who charged people to watch her draw and sew, selling her work for three guineas a piece. At one of the fairs she came to the attention of the Earl of Morton who recognised her talent as a painter, the earl became her sponsor, paying for her to have private lessons from William Craig, a Royal Academy painter, eventually becoming a member of the Royal Academy herself. Morton introduced Sarah into his circle of friends where she became much sought after as a painter of miniature portraits; she was even commissioned to paint Queen Victoria and other members of the Royal Family.

As a result Sarah became very successful and with the help of her benefactor she set up a studio in Bond Street, London. Such was her fame that Charles Dickens mentioned her in his novels, "Martin Chuzzlewit" and "Nicholas Nickleby."

Tragedy struck however, when in 1827 the Earl died and with that came the end of her sponsorship. Her health was also beginning to fail and as she was finding it increasingly difficult to continue painting she ran into financial difficulties. However Queen Victoria awarded her a pension from the civil list and with that she was able to retire.

Sarah moved to Liverpool where she married and came to live at No. 8 Duke Street. She stayed there until her death in1850 at the age of sixty six. Sarah was buried in St.James cemetery and with some searching her gravestone can be found.

Kitty Wilkinson 1786-1860

A woman of more humble beginnings from William Huskisson, Kitty Wilkinson was born in Londonderry. As a small girl her family made plans to move to Liverpool for a better life. On the journey across, at the entrance to the Mersey, the ship struck Hoyle Bank and sank. Among those who drowned were Kitty's father and sister; Kitty and her mother were left to struggle on with their new life in a strange city.

At the age of twelve Kitty went to work in a cotton mill in Caton, Lancashire, where she later married. Sadly her husband died leaving her with two small children and a frail mother to support.

After her mother's death Kitty moved back to Liverpool where she met and married Tom Wilkinson.

In 1832 there was a cholera outbreak in Liverpool and as the only owner of a copper boiler in her street, Kitty made it available to her neighbours. As a result of being able to boil and disinfect their clothes and bedding it was noted that the infection was kept under control in that neighbourhood. Kitty's cellar had been transformed into the first public wash-house.

As a result of the cholera outbreak many children were left orphaned, but thanks to Kitty and Tom's generosity and compassion, many children were cared for by them and given a basic education which became the nucleus of the first infants school to be established in Liverpool.

Kitty died in 1860 at the age of seventy three. Her gravestone can be found in St. James cemetery near to Huskisson's grand mausoleum.

Kitty Wilkinson is immortalised in the form of a stained glass window in the Lady Chapel of the Anglican Cathedral. The windows commemorate those extraordinary women who gave so much to the poor of the city. There are also plans to erect a statue of her which will be installed in St. Georges Hall. Kitty Wilkinson will be the first female to be commemorated within the building clearly a woman who is still highly regarded in Liverpool for her generous spirit.

The Oratory

This Grade 1 listed building was once the chapel of St.James cemetery and was used for funeral services before the burials took place within the grounds. Built in 1827 and designed by John Foster it takes the form of a Greek Doric Temple. At each end is a portico with six columns. There are no windows in the walls of the building but light enters from above. The interior houses a collection of statues and funereal monuments which have come from demolished churches within Liverpool. Amongst the monuments are those of the Nicholson family dating from 1834. A monument to Major General William Earle by the sculptor John Gibson. Welsh born but raised and educated in Liverpool his early talent as a sculptor came to the notice of William Roscoe who encouraged him to develop his skills. Gibson was commissioned by the widow of William Huskisson to carve a statue of her dead husband. This once stood outside the Custom House until it was later moved to Pimlico Gardens in London. Further examples of his work can be seen in the Walker Art Gallery.

There is a statue of Agnes Jones the "Angel of Mercy" as she was known in the city because of her work as a nurse in the Brownlow Hill Workhouse where she helped to improve the conditions of care for the poorest people. She died at the early age of thirty five from typhus.

A window in the Lady Chapel of the Anglican Cathedral also commemorates her work.

The Oratory is now part of the National Museums and Monuments on Merseyside.

A more modern and controversial work stands at the entrance to the Oratory. Commissioned by the B.B.C. for the 2005 Arts Festival, it is a piece by Tracy Emin, "The Roman Standard" it is made up of a thirteen foot high pole on top of which is perched a small bronze sparrow.

Some time after its installation the bird was stolen. An anonymous call to local Radio Merseyside telling of the whereabouts of the sparrow led to its discovery in the grounds of the Oratory.

A note attached to it confessing that "we would have returned it sooner but we were scared" to which Tracy Emin replied "this is taking the p... don't bite the hand that feeds."

Hillsborough Memorial

There is a plaque on the plateau of the Anglican Cathedral.

The inscription on it is a poignant reminder of the 1989 football tragedy

when ninety six people lost their lives, crushed against the front barriers at

Sheffield Wednesday's stadium during a football match on April 15th 1989.

It has the inscription "**You'll Never Walk Alone,**"

the anthem of Liverpool football supporters.

Hope Street

Named after William Hope, a merchant whose house once stood on the site of which is now occupied by the Liverpool Philhramonic Hall. Either end of the street stand the two cathedrals, the Anglican Cathedral, designed by Gibert-Scott in the Gothic style, and the modern looking Metropolitan Cathedral which was designed by Sir Frederick Gibberd. Both architects were chosen as a result of competitions. A little further along Hope Street are two fifteen foot tall bronze sculptures, commissioned by the Liverpool Echo and paid for through public donations. The bronzes show representations of the Archbishops of the two Cathedrals, Archbishop Warlock and Bishop David Sheppard. The two religious leaders worked together to break down the religious differences between the two faiths; each man is placed looking towards their respective Cathedrals.

Among the buildings of interest along Hope Street and standing on the corner of Falkner Street is the Grade II listed building of Blackburne House which has had quite a history. Originally built in 1788 for John Blackburne a wealthy salt refiner and supporter of the slave trade. The house was later bought by George Holt, a cotton broker and an abolitionist and who was also a supporter of womens rights. Holt opened the house in 1844 as a girls school. Blackburne House School for Girls continued as a school until its closure in1986. The building re-opened in 1994 as The Womens Technology and Education Centre.

Brian Epstein, manager of the Beatles rented a flat at no. 36 Falkner Street and the Liverpool poet and painter Adrian Henri lived at no. 24 opposite Blackburne House. He also taught for a time at Liverpool College of Art. This Grade II listed building is currently owned by the John Moores University. Among its former students were John Lennon, Cynthia Lennon, Stuart Sutcliffe... and myself!

The art college had its origins as part of the Liverpool Institute Boys High School whose former pupils were George Harrison and Paul and Mike McCartney. The former school now houses the Liverpool Institute of Performing Arts or L.I.P.A. The idea for a school to develop the performing arts was set up by Sir Paul and Mark Featherestone-Witty This heavily subscribed college offers comprehensive courses in dance, music and drama as well as theatre management and performance technology.

A Case History

On the corner of Mount Street and Hope Street sits a collection of left luggage entitled "A Case History." created by John King. The set of suitcases have the names of organisations and celebrities relating to Liverpool. A plan of who's who is located on the nearby wall of what was once the Liverpool College of Art, now part of the John Moores University.

Amongst the many pieces of luggage is one belonging to Henry Booth, founder of the Liverpool - Manchester railway, which on its opening led to the demise of William Huskisson M.P for Liverpool.

Suitcases with the name tags of John Lennon and Paul McCartney sit alongside those of Roger McGough, Brian Pattern and Adrian Henri, Liverpool poets and artists. One suitcase which stands out for me is that of artist Sam Walsh. Born in Dublin, he moved to Liverpool and made it his home.One of the sixties Liverpool based artists. He also taught for a time at the Liverpool College of Art Foundation School in Hope Place, where he was very popular and well liked....Sam's work, "Pin-Up 1963- For Francis Bacon" can be seen at the Walker Art Gallery. Another painting of Paul McCartney, entitled "Mike's Brother," is on show at the National Portrait Gallery in London. Mike was once a member of the Liverpool satirical group "The Scaffold "and is also a highly talented photographer.

The Philharmonic Hall

This Grade II listed building is home to the Royal Liverpool Philharmonic Orchestra. The original hall, built in 1849 was destroyed by fire in 1933. Designed by Herbert Rowse in the style of Art Deco it took just six years to build. The final cost of the building came to £120,000 (5.51 million in today's terms). Herbert Rowes' fee came to £6,869 (equivalent to £120,000.)

In the entrance hall is a memorial plaque dedicated to John Frederick Clarke, a local viola player, and to the other members of the orchestra who lost their lives on the ill fated Titanic.

The Philharmonic Dining Hall

A Grade II listed building, the Philharmonic Pub, known locally as the "Phil" is a popular meeting place for the local students. Designed by Walter Thomas (not to be confused with Walter Aubrey Thomas) for Cain's Brewery, it was opened in 1894 and its style is that of Art Nouveau.

Ornate wrought iron gates bearing the motto and arms of Robert Cain give a flavour of the interior. The highly polished wooden mahogany bar the base of which is decorated in colourful mosaic design, wood paneling on the walls,mosaic flooring and stained glass windows. The tobacco stained ceiling is equally heavily decorated. Robert Cain is featured in a mosaic on the floor just beyond the main entrance.

There is one Grande Lounge and two smaller rooms named Brahms and Liszt. The Grand Lounge was once the billiard room and the two smaller were originally named the smoke room and news room.

To appreciate the interior, especially the mosaic floor and bar decoration, an early visit is recommended as the pub gets very busy.The Phil is also famous for its ornately furnished gents toilets, a tourist attraction in its own right, heavily tiled, with rose coloured marble urinals and wash basins which are in stark contrast to the ladies facilities which incidentally were only added in the forties reflecting the fact that the Phil was built for the purposes of gentlemen only.

Everyman Theatre

The original site held a chapel called Hope Hall, built in 1837 it was later converted to a concert hall and later still a cinema. The EverymanTheatre came into being in 1964. It was a very successful and innovative theatre with the works of local playwrights Alan Bleasdale and Willy Russell whose plays were given their debuts at the Everyman. In the basement was the Bistro which became popular with the local artists and musicians, including Arthur Dooley, Adrian Henri and Roger McGough.

The theatre closed in 2011 for major re-furbishment and is due to re-open in 2013.

Metropolitan Cathedral

At the opposite end of Hope Street from the Anglican Cathedral stands the Metropolitan Cathedral. The Cathedral came about as the result of a competition after the earlier design by Sir Edwin Lutyens proved too costly. Sir Frederick Gibberd's design was chosen but Lutyen's crypt was incorporated into the new design. Construction began in1922 and within just five years was completed. Known locally as Paddies Wig-Wam because of its shape, it caused great controversy when it was first built but it has since become part of the iconic Liverpool landscape.

The steps to the Cathedral are flanked by coloured glass columns which were designed by a German artist, Raphael Seitz. At the top of the main steps and above the entrance sits the bell tower in which are housed four bells, named Mathew, Mark, Luke and John. The stone bell tower is inscribed with stylised crosses. The largest cross being that of Christ and the two either side those of the thieves who were crucified with Him; one cross shows the tears of the repentant.

On either side of the main entrance are two sliding doors made of bronze.

The Mayan-like designs are in fact the emblems of the the four saints. The man of St.Mathew, the lion of St. Mark, the ox of St. Luke and the eagle of St.John.

The circular nave and central high altar is the focal point of the interior and it gives a very powerful image of the altar as the aisles and seats fan out around it. Above the central altar is a bronze figure of Christ, created by Dame Elizabeth Frink, she also designed the "Risen Christ" which is above the west door of the Anglican Cathedral.

Fourteen of the Cathedral's buttresses hold the stations of the cross; cast in bronze they are the work of Sean Rice who is also responsible for the lectern and statues of Abraham in the West Apse and Shemaiah in the crypt.

Around the nave are the chapels each with its own distinctive chararcter. The Chapel of the Blessed Sacrament contains a statue by Arthur Dooley of the risen Christ.

At the entrance to the Chapel of Relics in the crypt, is a doorway carved from marble. It has a mechanism which enables it to roll open and close, alluding to the stone which sealed the tomb of Christ. The chapel also houses the tombs of the three former Archbishops of Liverpool.

Within the Chapel of Rememberance is The Golden Book in which the names of the people who had contributed to the cost of the Cathedral are remembered. So far seventeen volumes have been completed with over 5000,000 names inscribed.

Against the exterior wall of the north side of the Cathedral is a plain wooden cross and beneath this an altar. This large plaza area is used for outdoor services.

The coronet tower with its stylised crown of thorns, has the largest stained glass panels in the world; the red, yellow and blue colours which are thrown down into the interior represent the Holy Trinity.

The architect of the university was Liverpool born Alfred Waterhouse. Known as "Slaughterhouse Waterhouse" because of his use of blood red terracotta bricks and tiles. Money for the construction of the building was raised by public appeal and private donations. One of the major donors was Henry Tate who had made his fortune from sugar refining. The university was formerly opened in 1892. The Victoria Building has since been converted into a museum and gallery, its impressive interior has been preserved.

Alftred Waterhouse also designed the former North Western Hotel which stands in front of Lime Street Station. This has since been bought by the John Moores University and converted into student accomodation.

Sitting behind the Metropolitan Cathedral on Brownlow Hill is the Victoria Building. The original redbrick university in the country (although Birmingham, Bristol, Leeds, Sheffield and Manchester are also referred to as the original redbrick universties!) The term was coined by Liverpool University professor, Edgar Allison Peers.

Rodney Street

Rodney Street takes its name from Admiral Rodney (1718-1792) A British Naval Officer best known for his role in the American War of Independence.

With over sixty Grade II listed houses and one church along the street, Rodney Street is a fine example of Georgian architecture, with a wide variety of designs of transom windows along the length of the street. Rodney Street is recognised as the equivalent of London's Harley Street due to the number of doctors and specialists who have their consulting rooms here.

Running parallel to Hope Street it was laid out between 17873-1784 by William Roscoe at one time M.P. for Liverpool and a passionate campaigner for the abolition of the slave trade. The first house to be completed was no.35, and was lived in by the Roscoe family.

There are many plaques along the length of the street to other distinguished residents,amongst them, Henry Booth the founder of the Liverpool-Manchester Railway who lived at no.34.

William Gladstone was born at no.62. Gladstone's father having made his vast fortune exporting sugar from his plantations in Jamaica and Demerara. William Gladstone went on to have a distinguished career in politics and was four times Prime Minister.

Liverpool born Dr. William Henry Duncan was born at no.54. He became interested in the health of the poor and started researching the living conditions of his patients. Duncan recognised that there was a link between housing conditions and the outbreak of diseases such as cholera, smallpox and typhus. Through his work he went on to become Liverpool's first Officer for Health and was also Britain's first Chief Medical Officer; one of the buildings in the Faculty of Medicine at Liverpool University is named after him.

James Maury the U.S. consul to Liverpool between 1790-1829, lived at no.4. Much later the house was used as a private nursing home and in September 19th 1934 Brian Epstein, The Beatles manager was born there.

Arthur Clough, poet and at one time personal assistant to Florence Nightingale, his wife's cousin, was born at no.9. His suffragist sister, Anne Clough who went on to become the first principal of Newnham College, Cambridge was also born here.

The writer Nicholas Monsarrat was born at no.11 in 1910.

N0.59 was home and work place of local photographer Edward Chambre Hardman. When he died in 1988 the house and contents were given to the National Trust. An archive of over 200,000 images along with photographic equipment, business and personal correspondence are all preserved. The house is open to the public.

On Rodney Street Grade II listed St. Andrews Church was built with contributions from Scottish families who had moved to Liverpool and gone on to make their fortunes from investing in the newly developing railway system. The church was designed by Liverpool born architect, Sir John Foster.

Within its grounds stands one of my favourite monuments, an unusually shaped tomb belonging to one William McKensie. A successful civil engineer, amongst many of his contracts included the building of the tunnels between Edgehill and Lime Street stations. Mackensie was also a notorious gambler and during a run of bad luck one evening Mackensie promised his soul to the devil in return for a winning hand of poker. Some time after this pact he became ill and remembering his promise, he had a tomb built with enough space inside to fit a card table and chair. Upon his death he left instructions to have himself placed sitting at the card table holding a winning hand, in the hope of cheating the devil from claiming his soul! His ghost is said to haunt Rodney Street.

Roscoe Gardens

At the bottom of Mount Pleasant is a memorial to Renshaw Street Chapel situated within the Roscoe Memorial Gardens. The memorial is on the site of a chapel which once stood on the site. Joseph Blanco White (1775-1841) and William Roscoe(1753-1831) were buried here and plaques to them can be found on the memorial.

Born Jose Maria Blanco Crespo, White was a Spanish poet and theologian, educated for the Catholic priesthood his religious doubts grew.

Born in Mount Pleasant to the son of a market gardener William Roscoe. At the age of twelve Roscoe left school to work in his father's garden, spending his spare time studying the classics and law, becoming a successful lawyer. He was briefly elected M.P.for Liverpool and became a strong abolitionist.On leaving politics Roscoe led a group of Liverpool botanists who went on to create the Liverpool Botanic Gardens in Mount Pleasant.

Roscoe fell into financial difficulties and was forced into bankruptcy. Many of his assets were sold, however a group of friends bought a number of books from his vast collection and donated them to the Liverpool Athenaeum.

Falkner Gardens

Named after Edward Falkner, soldier and Sheriff of Lancashire who in 1797 at the height of a threatened invasion from France, within twenty four hours he had gathered a fighting force of 1,000 men.

Built between 1830-1835 this is another Georgian Square and one of the city's first open spaces. Edward Falkner had bought the land as an investment but at the time the square was unpopular because of its distance from the town, it was given the name "Falkner's Folly." In later years however it became one of the most fashionable squares in the city with the private gardens being accessible only to the residents of the square.Nowadays it is freely accessible with well maintained herbaceous borders and mature plane trees.

At the eastern entrance to the gardens is a memorial to the Black Seamen who lost their lives during the Second World War.

Abercromby Square

By the late 18th century the area around Mount Pleasant and Brownlow Hill were being developed to house the wealthy Liverpool merchants who wanted to move out of the busy town centre to the more rural outskirts and cleaner air.

John Foster was appointed designer for the area and Abercromby Square was to be the central focus of the new development. The square was named after Sir Ralph Abercromby one time commander of the British Army in Eygpt who wasl was killed in the Battle of Alexandria in 1801.

Within the square there is a garden which features a domed Garden House. The garden square was surrounded by railings and locked gates for the use of the residents only. Nowadays however these gardens are open to the public and the square, along with the houses are entirely owned by the University of Liverpool. The square has some fine examples of Georgian houses and it is often used in films which are set in that period.

Chavasse Memorial

Abercromby Square holds a very touching memorial to Captain Noel Chavasse. The bronze memorial shows Captain Chavasse and a Liverpool Scottish stretcher bearer attending to a wounded soldier.

The son of the Bishop of Liverpool, Noel Chavasse was raised at no.19 Abercromby Square and studied medicine at the university.

Attached to the King's Liverpool Scottish Regiment as a surgeon during W.W.1, Lieutenant Chavasse rescued wounded soldiers from no man's land saving the lives of more then twenty men, for which he was awarded the Victoria Cross.

A second Victoria Cross was awarded posthumously for the rescue of wounded soldiers at Passchendale, where he was mortally wounded. Captain Chavasse is buried in the military cemetery at Brandhoek, his headstone bears a represntation of two Victoria Crosses.

Chavasse Park in the Liverpool One area is named after him.

At the eastern end of Abercromby Square is a piece of sculpture by Barbara Hepworth called "Squares with Two Circles." Made from bronze and sitting on a concrete base it is one of three,one is in Yorkshire Sculpture Park near Wakefield, and the third is in Nasher Sculpture Center in Dallas.

Commercial Quarter

Part of the World Heritage Centre, this is the oldest part of Liverpool. Once the site of Liverpool Castle, Castle Street, Water Street, Dale Street, Old Hall Street and Victoria Street are still the financial heart of Liverpool and they also house many impressive examples of architecture and monuments reflecting the wealth of the city through trade as a sea port. This area has more than one hundred buildings that are listed for their architectural and historical interest.

Around Old Hall street many new buildings have sprung up thus re-inforcing this district as the financial centre of Liverpool. Some of the tallest and most innovative buildings in the North West of England are within this small area. New Hall Place is the largest office building in Liverpool and Beetham Tower West standing 140 mts. high is also the tallest, with uninterrupted views across the city, the River Mersey and beyond.

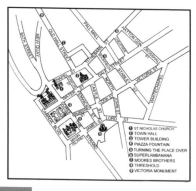

1 ST.NICHOLAS CHURCH
2 TOWN HALL
3 TOWER BUILDING
4 PIAZZA FOUNTAIN
5 TURNING THE PLACE OVER
6 SUPERLAMBANANA
7 MOORES BROTHERS
8 THRESHOLD
9 VICTORIA MONUMENT

Liverpool Town Hall

Built between 1749 and 1754, designed by John Wood, it was rebuilt in 1795 following a fire. A rear extension designed by James Wyatt was added in 1785. This Grade I listed building is also one of the oldest in the city centre. The sandstone for the building came from the quarry which is now the site of St. James cemetery. Friezes around the outside show elephants, crocodiles and African faces. The railings are decorated with elephants and pineapples, indications of Liverpool's trade with Africa and illustrating the goods that came into Liverpool.

On the dome of the Town Hall are four clocks flanked by lions and unicorns and sitting on top of the dome is a ten foot tall figure of the Roman goddess Minerva, made from terracotta and covered in gold leaf, she symbolises the wealth of the city and also acts as its protector.

At the back of the building, looking down on the Exchange Flags are four rather weather beaten figures representing the Four Seasons. These figures originally came from the Irish Houses of Parliament in Dublin.

Exchange Flags

At the heart of the commercial quarter is the Exchange Flags which has been the centre of the city's commerce for over seven hundred years. Situated behind the Town Hall, cotton traders struck deals outside on the flagstones. From the 1700's Exchange Flags was the site of the Liverpool cotton exchange, insurance and shipping business. The first cargo of cotton was unloaded in 1784,eight bales in total but by the end of the 1800's half a million bales were arriving from America alone. By the 1850's cotton accounted for almost half of the city's trade. Despite there being an Exchange building, traders preferred to do business outside on the flags and this continued into the late 1800's. A purpose built Exchange was opened in 1906 in Old Hall street.

Nelson Monument

In the centre of the square is a monument to Lord Nelson, paid for by public funds, a major contributor was William Roscoe, a Liverpool born historian and anti-slave campaigner. Unveiled in 1813 it shows four French prisoners-of-war in chains, each man representing Nelson's four victories over France. Cape Vincent, The Nile, Copenhagen and Trafalgar. A guardian angel, a sailor, a war hero and Britannia surround a canon, while

a skeleton peers beneath a draped flag. Around the base is Nelson's famous signal given at the Battle of Trafalgar,

"England expects that every man will do his duty".

Newsroom War Memorial

In a niche between the arches leading into Tithebarn Street, is a memorial dedicated to the Exchange workers who lost their lives during W.W.1. Joseph Parker was the sculptor and the model for the soldiers is believed to have been James Williams, a Liverpool boxer and grandfather of my brother-in-law!

Either side of this memorial are two columns on top of which sit figures, one depicting mother and child and the other depicts father and child. These pieces were designed by Austrian sculptor Siegfried Charoux.

Bank of Liverpool

At No7 Water Street stands the building of what was once the Bank of Liverpool. The large metal doors have two lifesize heads of a tiger, mouth open, carved in bronze. Why a tiger as a Liverpool bank's emblem? This particular bank absorbed Grindley's Bank which once handled a fortune in Indian and Eastern business. It is said that if you rub the fang of the sacred tiger it will bring you good luck. The tooth has been rubbed and polished so often now that it gleams like burnished gold.

Martin's Bank

Although it was the height of the depression in the thirties, no expense was spared in the building and interior design of Martins Bank. The original bank dates from the sixteenth century as a branch of the London bank that was begun by Sir Thomas Gresham. In 1918 the bank aquired The Bank of Liverpool which in turn had earlier bought Heywoods Bank. Heywoods Bank had first been established by brothers Arthur and Benjamin Heywood who had made their fortune from the slave trade. The building that we see today was built in 1928, designed by the architect Herbert Rowse. He took his inspiration from early Greek and Roman Art.

On either side of the imposing entrance are reliefs showing two small African children holding money bags, an anchor and a sextant, suggesting  the trading links to the sea and also possiby a reminder of the Heywood brothers beginnings and source of their wealth. Around the childrens' wrists and ankles are what appear to be bangles but which could also be interperated as manacles. Towering over them is Neptune, Roman god of the sea, whose "hands" rest firmly on their heads as though he is holding them down.

Reliefs of a liver bird and grasshopper can be seen on the exterior walls, this was once the logo of Martin's Bank with the grasshopper being taken from the Gresham family crest and the liver bird the emblem of the old Bank of Liverpool. In 1969 Martin's Bank was bought by Barclays.

During W.W.II the bulk of England's gold reserve was stored in the vaults of Martins Bank; a plaque on the wall in Rumford Street gives a short explanation.

India Building

This Grade II listed building was built between 1924-32 for Alfred Holt's shipping company the Blue Funnel Line. Herbert Rowse was the architect who was also responsible for the design of Martin's Bank, also in Water Street. The building takes up a whole block and is one of the largest office blocks in the city. It was designed to be converted into warehouse space if the office space had been difficult to let.

The most striking feature is the vaulted ceiling of the arcade which runs through the centre of the buildiing, this corridor is occupied by small shops.

Oriel Chambers

Designed by a young Liverpool Architect Peter Ellis in 1864 as a result of a competition. It was an innovative design at the time and one that caused a great deal of controversy, being described as "a great abortion" and "an agglomeration of great glass bubbles" In the style of the Modern Movement, the oriel windows allow a lot more light into the offices. This Grade I listed building was also the first metal structured building in the world.

Piazza Fountain

Off Water Street, in Drury Lane and running parallel to the Strand is the Goree Piazza, Goree being the name of an island off the coast of Senegal, which acted as a base for the slave trade. The piazza now houses a water feature, Piazza Fountain, also known as the Bucket Fountain. Next to it is an African shield upon which is a description of the fountain.

Designed by Richard Huws and made at Cammell Laird the shipbuilders who were based at Birkenhead. The buckets fill with water and as they fill and overflow the buckets tip and the water pours back into the pool.

At one time the water was switched off following complaints from office workers that the noise reminded them of flushing toilets. It is now sadly only in operation occassionally.

Moorfields

Tucked away in Moorfields at Cross Keys House, in which Yates Wine Lodge once operated, there is a piece of artistic engineering created by Richard Wilson. Commissioned in 2008 for the Biennial Arts Festival it is an eight metre diameter ovoid cut out of the façade, hydraulic apparatus within the building enables this section to rotate, moving inside out and upside down, the piece is aptly called "Turning the place Over."

Rigbys

No Commercial Quarter would be complete without a mention of the public houses within the area, many business deals being struck over a drink. A couple pubs worth a mention are "The Hole in the Wall" and "Rigby's."

Rigby's pub also dating from 1726 takes its name from Thomas Rigby (1815-1886), a successful wine and spirit merchant in the city who went on to become alderman. One of the pub's claim to fame is that Lord Nelson was a frequent customer in the 1790's!

"The Hole in the Wall" in Hackin's Hey, off Dale Street is said to be the oldest pub in Liverpool.The building dates from 1706 when it was a Quaker Meeting House, then 1726 the building changed hands and it became an inn. It is also not without its share of ghosts one of whom is said to be that of a Spanish sailor of the eighteenth century who was stabbed to death for refusing to take the King's shilling. The interior of The Hole in the Wall captures its age with tiny rooms, wood panelling and stained glass windows. A fine brass fireplace describes the pub's antiquity.

Irwell Chambers

Irwell Chambers is situated off Old Hall Street with entrances on two streets, Fazakerley and Union. A former office block, it takes its name from the Mersey and Irwell Canal which formed part of the Manchester Ship Canal. During renovation work on the building a sub basement was unearthed with steps that led down to tunnels beneath the street. On each side of the tunnels were cells, and the tunnel running from the south side runs beneath what is considered to be the oldest cobbled street in Liverpool. It is not known what the cells were used for but it has been suggested that they might have been holding cells for French prisoners of war or for victims of the slave trade.

Castle Street

One of the original streets of Liverpool, there is a spot in the road which marked the sanctuary stone within the precincts of the old Liverpool Fairs.

A plaque on the wall halfway down Castle Street directs you to the spot.

There are a number of Grade I and Grade II listed buildings in Castle Street, a number of which were once banks.

Adelphi Bank

On the corner of Castle Street and Brunswick Street is this Grade II Listed building. Designed by W.D. Caroe between 1891-92 it is constructed from pink sandstone and pale grey granite topped off with an ornate copper onion dome now green with age. The bronze entrance doors are the work of Thomas Stirling Lee who was also one of the main sculptors to have worked on the panel reliefs on St. George's Hall. These earlier reliefs had caused great controversy for its subject matter. The subject of the Adelphi doors is that of male friendship, taking examples from the Classics and the Bible. The Adelphi Bank merged with The Bank of Liverpool in 1899.

Bank of England

The Bank of England which was built between1845-48 as a branch of the Bank of England. Designed by C.R.Cockerell it is a mix of Greek and Roman Doric style.

At no. 60 Castle Street and Grade II listed was the Alliance Bank, later to be bought out by The North and South Wales Bank. It is now a hotel, the huge banking hall used as a bar and restaurant.

The National Westminster Bank built in 1900 and also Grade II listed was designed by Richard Norman Shaw, Willink and Thicknesse, the same partnership who had just completed the new headquarters of the White Star Line in James Street.

At the top end of Castle Street near the Town Hall is the British Foreign Marine Insurance Company Building. Dating from 1889 and Grade II listed, it was designed by G.E.Grayson. It has a heavily decorative mosaic frieze by Italian artist Salviati showing maritime scenes.

Hargreaves Building

Designed by Sir James Picton, Hargreaves Building stands on the corner of Covent Garden and Chapel Street.The building was designed for the banker Sir William Brown in 1859. The style is that of a Venetian palazzo. It has five bays facing Chapel Street and seven bays facing Covent Garden. Above the windows are carved busts of famous people who had contributed towards the exploration of the new world (the Americas) these include Columbus, Bermejo, Ferdinad, Isabella, Cortez and Pizarro.

William Brown was born in Ballymena, Ireland the son of an Irish linen merchant. The family moved to Maryland Baltimore where his father's business flourished. The company imported Irish linen and exported cotton and tobacco to Britain, both products were in great demand and as the company's wealth grew Alex Brown and Sons moved into merchant banking. William was sent to Liverpool in1809 to set up and run a branch of his father's firm, eventually setting up his own merchant bank under the company name Brown Shipley Bank. It financed merchants who were involved in shipping goods and slaves between Britain and the United States. Such was the success of the bank it was said that "There is hardly a wind that blows or a tide that flows in the Mersey, that does not bring a ship freighted with cotton or some other costly commodity to Mr. Brown's door".

William Browns business acumen was so trusted that during a financial crisis in 1837 he persuaded the Bank of England to loan his bank £2,000,000, an enormous amount, which he managed to repay within six months!

Brown was elected as Liberal M.P. for South Lancashire and held the seat from 1846-1859.

In 1860 William Brown presented Liverpool with a library and museum. He was made a baronet in1860 for his services to the city. He died in 1864 at the age of seveny nine and is buried in St. Jame's Cemetery.

The building takes its name from William Brown's son-in-law who ran the Liverpool business.

Tower Building

the Napoleonic Wars. In 1819 the Tower was demolished to allow for the widening Water Street. The present Tower has since been converted into apartments and units for commercial and retail use.

Another Grade II listed building the Tower building stands on the Strand opposite St. Nicholas Church and across the road from the Liver Building it was designed by the same architect, Walter Aubrey Thomas and it is one of the earliest steel framed buildings to be built in England. White glazed terracotta tiles were used in an attempt to deal with the polluted atmosphere. The architectural design reflects the earlier fortified building which previously stood on the site. The Tower replaces an earlier sandstone mansion and a later fortified house known as the Tower of Liverpool. The owners were the Stanley family who later took the title, Earl of Derby. That building was leased to Liverpool Corporation, part of it being converted into a prison, amongst whose inmates were French prisoners of war during

Superlambanana

One of Liverpool's most unusual public monuments is currently standing in Tithebarn Street, at the entrance to the John Moores University.

It began as a small plasticine model and it still manages to retain that simplicity despite its size. Superlambanana was created by Japanese artist Taro Chiezo who describes his work as a parody of genetic engineering. Superlambanana has had many offspring which can be seen scattered around the city. A small flock stand on the Strand near to the Cunard building.

Also at the top of Tithebarn Street was St Patrick's Cross, a spot where in 1432, St. Patrick gave his last sermon before leaving for Ireland.

Old Hall Street

In Old Hall Street is a life size bronze statue of John and Cecil Moore, John Moore created a betting system for football and later established Littlewoods stores. As a keen Everton supporter John Moore went on to become chairman of Everton Football Club.

After the Liverpool Polythecnic was given university status, it changed its name to the John Moores University thus ensuring John Moores name will be remembered.

Cotton Exchange

This Grade II listed office block in Old Hall street was built between 1905-06 to replace the former Cotton Exchange in Exchange Flags.The original facade by Matreat and Simpson was replaced between1967-69 with a design by the company of Newton, Dawson, Forbes and Tate. At the main entrance is a massive figure representing the River Mersey and in the courtyard are two more equally massive statues representing Commerce and Navigation. The statues had once been on the old Exchange Building but were taken down as they had deteriorated badly and were in danger of crashing to the ground.

Threshold

At the top of Old Hall street overlooking the River Mersey stands an impressive structure entitled "Threshold to the Ends of the Earth". It depicts thirty two faces of Liverpool people etched into glass portholes placed within the wall. The faces and names of the people highlight the diverse culture of the city.

Victoria Monument

Standing in Derby Square is the Grade II listed monument, once the site of Liverpool Castle; a plaque on the side of the monument shows a representatiion of the castle with a brief description of its history. The sculptor for this monument was C.J.Allen and the architect was F.M. Simpson who was also the first professor of architecture at Liverpool University, the monument was unveiled in 1902. The sculptures surrounding the base of the monument depict Agriculture, Commerce, Education and Industry, and above Wisdom, Justice, Charity and Peace. On top of the dome stands the figure of Fame.

At one time it housed a gents lavatory beneath its structure, rather deflating the grandeur of the subject. To make matters worse the statue brings a smile to many a Liverpudlian as the Queen is shown to be grasping a rather interestingly shaped sceptre...

Liverpool Castle

Built in the early 1230's by William de Ferres 4th Earl of Derby to protect the new port. It was built on the highest point overlooking the Mersey where the Victoria Monument now stands. The main castle consisted of a gatehouse facing Castle Street, with a tower either side of the gatehouse. Three more towers on the three remaining corners with a covered walk way connecting each tower. Inside the castle was a chapel, bake house and brew house with an orchard and dovecot running down to the river. A tunnel running underneath the dry moat led down to the river as a means of escape if the castle came under attack.

The castle came under attack only twice, once in 1315 and then much later in 1653, during the Civil War. Following the defeat of the Royalists by the Parliamentarians, orders were given to destroy the castle but only the gatehouse and parts of the defensive walls were taken down.

The castle changed hands many times until in 1715 an Act was passed to demolish the by now ruined remains. In1734 St.George's Church was built on the site; it was designed by Thomas Steers, the engineer of Liverpool's first dock. By 1825 that was pulled down and a new church was built, the architect for this church was John Foster.This stood until 1899 when that too was demolished to make way for the Victoria Monument.

In 1976 excavation of the site of the new Crown Courts uncovered a ditch which is believed to have been dug as part of the Civil War defences. It is also said that there are still tunnels running down to the river which were used as escape routes by the Parliamentarian soldiers during the Civil War.

Culture Quarter

In 2008 Liverpool was awarded European Capital of Culture, becoming the first city in England to be granted that title. This area has a number of museums and galleries, one of the oldest being the Walker Art Gallery and the World Museum of Liverpool being the largest with a diverse collection of exhibits.

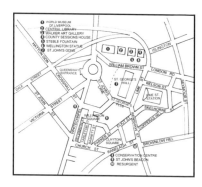

St. George's Hall takes pride of place and located behind it is St.John's Gardens, a memorial park and an oasis of peace.

St. John's Gardens

St. John's Gardens takes its name from St.John the Babtist Church and graveyard which once occupied the site, dating from 1767 it was used as the main burial grounds for the city. Work began on the construction of St. John the Baptist Church and was consecrated in 1784. The church and grounds were used until 1854 when the churchyard closed and the church was later demolished to make way for St. George's Hall.

During the Napoleonic Wars many French sailors were captured and sent to Liverpool where they were imprisoned in Liverpool Gaol which was housed in the Tower Building on the Strand. At one time more than 4,000 French P.O.W's were detained there under very poor conditions. As a consequence many prisoners died and their bodies were taken for burial in St. John's churchyard.

A plaque was erected at the base of the retaining wall of the gardens in 1924 by the French Government. An inscription in French and English reads:

"To her sons who died in captivity in Liverpool in 1772/1803 and whose bodies lie here in the old cemetery of St.John the Baptist. France ever grateful."

Each year the French Ambassador lays a wreath at the foot of the plaque.

The gardens, which opened in 1904 has a collection of statues of those people who made a major contribution to the city, as leaders and social reformers. Robert Hampson, mayor at the time stated "the statues would not only serve to commemorate worthy sons of Liverpool but would also act as an incentive to the younger generation."

William Gladstone 1809-1898

despite continual attention from many suitors, Penelope rejected them all and remained faithful. Gladstone's private life was taken up with rescuing ``fallen'' women, often putting himself in physical and moral danger, in his own words he ``courted evil,'' testing himself against temptation.

The Gladstone monument, designed by Sir Thomas Brock, is one of the largest in the gardens, it shows him standing holding a scroll and books. Seated either side of him are female figures representing Truth and Justice.

Born in Liverpool at 62 Rodney Street. Gladstone's father owned sugar plantations in the West Indies and made his fortune from trading with America and the West Indies.

Gladstone entered politics as a Liberal M.P. and became Prime Minister on four occasions. A scholar of Homer, he would have perhaps appreciated Jorge Prado's sculpture in Wolstenholme Square, entitled ``Penelope'' named after the wife of Odysseus.

There is a loose connection with Gladstone and Penelope in so far as, whilst her husband was away fighting in the Trojan Wars, and

William Rathbone 1819-1902

Following the death of his first wife, and grateful for the care that was given to her by a nurse, with the help of his friend Florence Nightingale, Rathbone was integral in setting up a district nursing system. He was elected as Liberal M.P for Liverpool and also helped to found what was later to become Liverpool University.

A great philanthropist, in 1891 William Rathbone was awarded Freeman of the City for his major contribution towards the improvement of the city and its people.

His plaque states "*A guardian of the poor for thirty years.*"

The statue was designed by George Frampton.

Born in Liverpool into a wealthy family of merchants and ship owners as mayor of Liverpool, William's father laid the foundation stone of St George's Hall.)

In partnership with his brother they continued the success by trading in the West Indies and later, during the American Civil War their fortune was made in the dangerous business of blockade running. William Rathbone used his profits from this to fund philanthropic works, thus following in his grandfather's footsteps, who was a great supporter of Kitty Wilkinson's campaign to establish public baths and wash houses.

Sir Arthur Forwood 1836-1898

Thomas Major Lester 1829-1903

Liverpool born ship owner, cotton trader and merchant Arthur Forwood was a member of the City Council and served as Mayor. A Conservative politician he became First Secretary to the Admirality and Privy Councillor. Forwood was involved in raising capital for the building of Liverpool Overhead Railway and was also Director of the Cunard Line and the Bank of Liverpool (St Martin's Bank.)

Designed by George Frampton.

Born in London, Thomas Lester studied theology at Christ College Cambridge and in 1853 became curate of St. Mary's Kirkdale. Apart from a brief time away from the city, he spent the rest of his life in Liverpool, becoming an Honorary Canon. Lester established the Major St. Ragged School, a girls home in Walton Road and also founded Stanley Hospital.

Thomas Major Lester is buried in Anfield cemetery and the inscription on his tombstone says:

``freely we serve because we freely love"

This statue was also designed by George Frampton.

Andrew Balfour 1824-1866

Born in Scotland and educated at St Andrews University. In 1884 Balfour moved to Liverpool and made it his adopted home. A great success in business enabled him to give generously to many deserving causes. Balfour founded the Duke Street Home to provide better living conditions for sailors, their families and orphans.

The statue was designed by Albert Bruce Joy.

Monsignor James Nugent 1822-1905

Liverpool born, he was ordained in 1845 and became priest of St. Nicholas Church in the same year. In 1860 Father Nugent was appointed chaplain for Walton gaol.

During the 1840's as a result of the Irish potato famine there was a great influx of Irish families into Liverpool. Nugent set up schools for the catholic children, a boys school in Rodney Street; founded the Catholic Institute in Hope Street and a refuge for ``fallen women.''

Nugent was made a monsignor in 1890. He is buried in Ford cemetery; an inscription on his monument says

``*Father of the orphan, refuge, of the outcast, friend of the imprisoned, saviour of fallen womanhood*''

The statue was designed by Frederick William Pomeroy.

Kings Liverpool Regiment

Taking central position in the gardens and the largest monument to the Kings Regiment, one of the oldest regiments in the British Army. The monument is made up of a bronze figure of Britannia with soldiers either side of her, one dressed in the regiment's original uniform and the other in contemporary uniform. The monument commemorates the regiment's service in the second Boer War in South Africa.

At the rear of the monument is a drummer boy of which smaller reproductions were later made and sold.

The statue was designed by William Goscombe John.

t. George's Hall.

A competition to design the Hall was won by a young London architect Harvey Lonsdale Elmes. Its foundation stone was laid in 1838 to commemorate Queen Victoria's coronation, however constuction did not begin until 1842. Elmes failing health forced him to withdraw from the supervision of the building and in 1847 he died. Sir Charles Cockerell was appointed as architect. Cockerell was responsible for the majority of the interior design. The building was opened to the public in 1854. Neo-Classical in style with Greek and Roman references, it is reputed to be the largest Neo-Classical building in Europe.

The bronze doors have the letters SPQL (The Senate and the People of Liverpool), drawing a comparison to SPQR which was the badge of the Holy Roman Empire.

The south entrance was re-designed from the original plans, instead of an entrance into the basement, steps were built up the outside of the South Portico. After some years these were taken away and replaced by a podium which meets the street line. The granite columns were used as the gate piers for the entrance to Sefton Park. The stone balustrades were taken and re-positioned outside the Museum and Library on William Brown Street.

A Grade I Listed building, St.George's Hall combines law courts and a concert hall,which holds the second largest organ in Europe. It was also the first public building in the U.K to have air conditioning installed, engineered by Sir David Boswell Reid who was later to install air conditioning in the Houses of Parliament.

A set of reliefs were added between 1882 and 1901 along the Eastern façade.These were designed by Thomas Stirling Lee, C.J.Allen and Conrad Dressler. The original plan was to have been for twenty eight panels, but only twelve were completed. The first panels by Thomas Stirling Lee, entitled ``The Attributes and Results of Justice'' caused the biggest outcry. The child and young girl in the reliefs are portrayed without clothes, which resulted in the commission being cancelled. It took six years before the committee agreed to the completion of four more panels. A further six were produced by C.J. Allen and Conrad Dressler.

At the foot of the steps of St. George's Hall stands the city's cenotaph, designed by Lionel Budden and sculpted by George Tyson -Smith.It was unveiled on Armistice Day November 11th 1930 by the Earl of Derby. In front of the cenotaph sit four stone lions dating from 1858, they were designed by Charles Cockerell and sculpted by William Nichol.

Of all the famous trials that were held at St. George's Hall the trial of Florence Elizabeth Maybrick still attracts debate over the verdict.

In May of 1889 Florence Maybrick was charged with the murder by arsenic poison of her cotton broker husband James Maybrick. She was convicted and sentenced to death but at the last minute the sentence was changed to one of penal servitude for life. She was released in January 1904, after serving fifteen years, returning to her native America where she died in 1941, alone and penniless.

Florence returned to Liverpool only once, to attend the Grand National.

Walker Art Gallery

The Walker Art Gallery is named after Sir Andrew Barclay Walker a successful businessman whose great wealth came from the family brewing business. Sir Andrew Walker went on to become Mayor of Liverpool. To commemorate his time as mayor he gifted the Art Gallery to Liverpool at a cost of over £40,000. The Walker Art Gallery was officially opened in September 1877 and it houses the largest collection of art outside London. The collection dates from 1819 when William Roscoe donated thirty seven paintings, the first aquisitions to go on public display.

Amongst the collection are a number of paintings Liverpool artist George Stubbs (1724-1806) chiefly self taught, he was most noted for his portraits of horses, "Horse frightened by a Lion" in the Gallery shows his expertise in the anatomical detail of the horse. Perched on top of the Building sits the Spirit of Liverpool, looking towards the city. This is a replica of the original figure which was removed in 1993 as the marble had deteriorated badly and was in danger of crashing through the roof.

Carved in marble by John Warrington it shows her in a Britannia like pose sitting on a bale of cotton She is wearing a laurel wreath on her head and holding a trident and a steamship propeller in each hand. A liver bird sits by her left arm and at her feet, an artist's palette, compass and set square, symbolising trade and the arts of the city.

The Spirit of Liverpool was positioned into place on the roof of the new gallery in 1877. The replica was carved out of a block of Chinese marble and was hoisted into position in 1994.

The original Spirit is now in the National Conservation Centre. Because of its sheer size the statue had to be installed before the main doors to the building could be fitted.

Steble Fountain

This is a replica of the original Steble Fountain which was designed by W. Cunliffe and made for the Paris Exhibition of 1867. The original is now in Massachusetts, three other copies are to be found in Bordeaux, Geneva and Lyon.

The fountain was a gift to the city by its namesake Colonel Steble, Mayor of Liverpool in 1876.

Beneath the foundation stone is a glass bottle containing newspapers and silver coins.

Sometimes filled with detergent by the jokers of the town, a bizarre sight to see as the bubbles and foam cascade down and overflow onto the pavement.

Wellington Column

Designed by George Anderson Lawson The column was built to commemorate Wellington's victories during the Napoleonic Wars, it stands at 132' and the panels around the base show scenes of the battle of Waterloo. Pre metric measurements of length are inscribed around the column with more set into a bronze plaque which is set into one of the plinths. Running from the plinth, set into the pavement is a long brass strip showing a one hundred foot measurement and a chain of one hundred links.

Standing on top of the plinth is the 14' high figure of Wellington. It was cast from the cannon which had been captured at the Battle of Waterloo.

Liverpool Resurgent

Not strictly in the Culture Quarter but worthy of a mention, this statue by Sir Jacob Epstein was commissioned by the directors Lewis's department store. It was named "Resurgence" as a sign of the city's re-birth after the destruction of large parts of the city during W.W.II.

The bronze figure of a naked man standing on the prow of a ship is a favourite meeting place. Its official name is "Liverpool Resurgence" but it is known locally as "Dickie Lewis"

The three reliefs above the store's main entrance were also designed by Epstein. They show children at play, reflecting the new generation of post –war children. The baby in the pram was modelled on his granddaughter, Annabel, by his daughter Kitty and Lucien Freud. Epstein's pet dog, Frisky sits beside the pram.

Liverpool Empire Theatre

Across the road from the Walker, on Lime Street stands the Liverpool Empire Theatre. It is the second theatre to be built on this site and it opened in 1925. It boasts the largest two tier auditorium in Britain and can seat 2,350 people. Designed by W. and T.R. Milburn for Moss Empires, the interior decoration was carried out by E.O. Griffiths. The theatre is Grade II listed.

Amongst the many performers who have appeared at the Empire, were the Beatles. First performing there in 1962, and returning in 1965 to give their final concert in Liverpool.

The theatre is also said to be haunted, one is that of a young girl in Victorian dress and a second ghost is that of a former painter at the theatre called Len!

There is another interesting feature of the theatre on the outside wall, on Nelson Street, inscribed in the portland stone are initials and the date Aug 23rd 1923.

St.John's Beacon

Built in 1968 at a height of 133 mts St.John's Beacon was built as a ventilation shaft for St.John's market but it was never used. It also housed a revolving restaurant and observation deck. The tower is no longer open to the public but it is home to local radio station Radio City.

This area takes in Duke Street, College Lane and the Bluecoat Chambers. It was the first area in Liverpool to be developed due to its close proximity to the port. The area is named after the long narrow lanes or ropewalks which were used for the laying out of materials prior to them being twisted into rope. Bold Street was recognised as the ideal length of a standard length for a British Naval Rope being 305m. Bold Street was named after Jonas Bold, a slave trader, sugar merchant and banker who went on to become Mayor of Liverpool in 1802. Other trades connected with ship building sprang up in this area and soon merchants began to build their homes here to be near to their businesses. Duke Street, Hanover and Bold Streets were the first streets to be developed followed by the connecting streets of Fleet and Seel Street. An assortment of buildings sprung up as the area became more populated. Merchants built shops with living quarters above, warehouses and private Georgian houses for the wealthy traders and sea captains were built around gardens and squares such as Cleveland Square and Wolstenholme Square. One example which is still standing was the home and warehouse of Thomas Parr, a slave trader and banker. Standing on the corner of Colquitt and Parr Street it later became the home for the Royal Institution.

There are further examples of 18th and 19th century buildings along the length of Bold Street.

The Lyceum Club at the bottom of Bold Street was built between 1800-1802 to the design of Thomas Harrison. It was built for the purpose of a gentlemens club and lending library. It was still in use up until 1942 when the building was taken over for use by the city's head post office.

69

St. Luke's Church

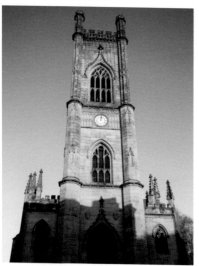

At the top of Bold Street, on the corner of Berry Street and Leece Street stands St. Luke's Church known locally as "the bombed out church" it stands on a plot of land formerly owned by Jonas Bold; The original design was by John Foster Snr. Begun in 1802 and completed by his son John Foster in 1831, having changed his father's design. During the Second World War St. Luke's was hit by an incendiary bomb. The remaining shell of the church has been left as an unofficial war memorial, its interior shows the fire damaged, blackened beams with some of the skeletal windows still retaining traces of the stained glass.

The church yard is a public garden now and within the grounds is a memorial to the victims of the Irish Potato Famine.

The church interior is host to a range of events from film, music and art, organised by Urban Strawberry Lunch a Liverpool based group who make all of their instruments from re-cycled materials after their own were destroyed in a fire. The group are heavily involved in community projects at St. Luke's bringing life back into the church.

Banksy

At the top of Duke Street, and on the corner of Berry Street, painted on the wall of a disused pub is a piece of official graffiti by Banksy. Commissioned for the 2004 Liverpool Biennial the piece caused much controversy then and still continues to do so today with the council. At one point the council went so far as to board it over during the year when Liverpool was awarded the City of Culture as they believed it to be an eyesore.

There is some dispute as to whether the creature is a rat or a cat and whether it is holding a machine gun or a marker pen. I believe it is a rat armed with a marker pen, hence the red stripes which lead around the building.In fact earlier photos of this graffiti show the marker pen with a red tip but this has since broken off.

The Imperial Arch

A little further along Berry Street at the top of Nelson Street,is the Liverpool Imperial Arch.Standing at the entrance to China Town, home of one of the oldest Chinese communities in Europe at over fifteen metres high it is the largest arch outside of China.

Built in Shanghai, a twin town of Liverpool, it was brought over and re-constructed in accordance with fengshui by eight Shanghai workers, the arch was unveiled in the year 2000. It has an inscription, "Zhong Guo Cheng," which translated means "China Town".

The arch is decorated with Chinese writing and two hundred dragons, twelve of whom are pregnant, a Chineses sign of good fortune. The arch is protected on either side by three pairs of temple lions of fu-dogs.

The five colours used to decorate the arch relate to the five Chinese elements. Yellow (earth), red (fire), green (wood), white (metal) and black (water).

Penelope

Halfway down Duke Street is a passageway that leads into Wolstenholme Square the first enclosed gardens to be developed in Liverpool. Here is a modern construction by Cuban artist Jorge Pardo, entitled Penelope it is one of the most unusual and colourful sculptures,

comprising of twisted metal "stalks" with coloured plexi glass balls attached, taking on a magical look at night when it is illuminated. The structure takes its name after Penelope who was the wife of Odysseus. In Homer's "Odyssey" Penelope remained faithful to her husband while he was away fighting in the Trojan Wars.

The Royal Institution Building

Dating from 1799 this building in Colquitt Street was once the home and workplace of Thomas Parr, a successful slave trader and banker. The property was bought and set up in 1814 for the "promotion of Literature, Science and the Arts" William Rathbone IV, William Corrie and William Roscoe were among the founders. Arts and science courses were held there as well as it housing an art gallery and science museum. It was very successful until the Walker Art Gallery, Picton Library and Museums were opened in the 1860's and 1870's. Many of the paintings and science specimens from the Institution were donated to the Walker and Science Museum. The Institution was finally dissolved in 1948.

Thomas Parr's name lives on with a street named after him and a recording studio in Parr Street takes his name.

Fact

FACT Foundation for Art and Technology is based in the heart of the Ropewalks in Wood street running parallel to Bold Street. Incorporating a cinema and media galleries it plays a major role in promoting new forms of art in Liverpool.

The Alma de Cuba

In Seel Street, a former church is now operating as a restaurant and bar. Once St. Peter's Catholic Church it first opened in 1788 and did not close until 1978. It was later used by the local Polish community and as a result became known as the "Polish Church"

During redevelopment the remains of twenty two bodies, (eight monks and fourteen lay people) were discovered in the crypt, along with the body of a Fr.Bede Brewer.Fr.Brewer and the monks remains were re-interred at Ampleforth Abbey; the remains of the lay people were re-interred in Ford Cemetery.

Reconciliation

Designed by Stephen Broadbent, there were three identical statues of ``Reconciliation'', one each in Liverpool, Glasgow and Belfast. The meaning behind the statues is to recognise and tolerate religious differences. Two further statues have since been placed in Cotonou, Benin and Richmond Virginia, connecting Liverpool to the slave trade triangle and attempting to acknowledge the impact that the trade had on people's lives.

Tango.

This modern structure by British artist Allen Jones is to be found off Bold street in Concert Square. Made from coloured polychrome steel plates it shows two people entwined and merging into each other as they dance the Tango. Commissioned for the International Garden Festival of 1984 it was re-located to Concert Square when the festival closed. A further example of Allen Jones work can be seen in the Walker Art Gallery. Entitled "Hermaphrodite" it is in a similar style to "Tango" with male and female figures fused together. Allen jones was a central figure in the pop- art movement of the sixties and caused outrage with the femininst movement who accused him of objectify women after he produced pieces of furniture sculpures of fibre glass models of semi-naked women. Created in 1969 they are now accepted as important and valuable pieces of the pop- art movement.

Bluecoat Chambers

The Bluecoat School situated in School Lane was founded in 1708 by Bryan Blundell, a wealthy master mariner and slave trader and Rev.Robert Styth, Rector of St. Nicholas Church. It was dedicated to the "promotion of Christian Charity and training of poor boys in the principles of the Anglican Church." A Latin inscription of this is above the main entrance as a reminder of its original purpose. The schools' intake grew so rapidly that within ten years a new building, the present Bluecoat opened and a school remained there until 1906 when it re-located to Wavetree. The Bluecoat was saved from demolition in 1907 by Lord Leverhulme, the soap magnate. It is the oldest Grade I listed building in the centre of Liverpool, it now houses an art gallery, performance space, specialist shops and is used as an arts venue to promote new talent.

Athenaeum

Founded in 1797 the Athenaeum originated as a gentlemen's club and a meeting place for merchants and professional men of the city in order to exchange news and views on the affairs of the day. The original building was designed by John Foster. Amongst its founder members were William Roscoe, Dr. Duncan and Henry Booth; other members included James Maury America's first consul to Liverpool, John Gladstone, father of George Gladstone, all of whom lived in Rodney Street, and Francis Chavasse, Bishop of Liverpool who lived in Abercromby Square. The building was demolished in the 1920's to make way for the road widening of Church Street. Harold Dod was chosen to design the current building and it opened in 1924, Its location in Church Alley, off School Lane and Church Street can be easily overlooked.

The Liverpool Athenaeum predates the London Athenaeum which says much for the importance of Liverpool in the 18th century. Its library has grown to be one of the main resources for the history of the region and the club is still going strong today.

Bridewell

Located in Argyle Street at the lower end of Duke Street stands the Bridewell or police station. Dating from the 1850's it was used as an over night lock-up prior to the next morning's court appearance. On a visit to Liverpool during his book reading tours and doing research for a future book,"The Uncommercial Traveller" Charles Dickens paid a visit to the bridewell and was made an honorary constable. Liverpool was his next favourite city next to London. He wrote that "Liverpool lies in my heart next only to London".

James Newlands (1813-1871)

Born in Edinburgh, the son of a ropemaker James Newlands became Britain's first Borough Engineer in Liverpool, he engineered the world's first integrated sewage system, ten years before Joseph Bazalgette in London. He worked closely with Dr. Duncan in improving public health in the city.

Mathew Street

Mathew Street began life as a simple cart track back in the 1600's on land that was owned by a Mathew Pulckington, a local squire.At that time the natural pool of Liverpool came up as far as Whitechapel. Pulckington's land proved to be an ideal spot to build warehouses as goods could be unloaded directly from the ships. These buildings were to form the foundations of the later brick built warehouses some of which still stand along Mathew Street. Flanagan's Apple pub for example was once a warehouse which stored apples.

Within a short time Pulckington's Alley developed into a busy thoroughfare and was renamed Mathew Street, taking Pulckington's Christian name.

Once the wholesale fruit and vegetable market, the Cavern Quarter has become synonymous with the Beatles and wherever you move there are constant reminders of their prescence, there is even a Beatles themed hotel in the quarter the "Hard Day's Night." The Beatles looking down from the hotel on the street below were sculpted by local artist Dave Webster.

Lined with bars, clubs and pubs Mathew Street is the main street within the Cavern Quarter.The Victorian pubs, The White Star and The Grapes are two of the oldest in the area. The Grapes is probably the more well known of the two because of its Beatles association. As the Cavern only sold soft drinks at the time and the Grapes being the nearest to the club it was the pub frequented by most of the groups who played there.The back room is crammed with Beatles memorabilia and photos. One in particular shows them seated at a bench, drinks in hand. The bench is still there along with an original piece of wallpaper, preserved behind protective glass.

❶ CAVERN CLUB
❷ JOHN LENNON
❸ WALL OF FAME
❹ ELEANOR RIGBY

The back room of the White Star is reputed to be where the Beatles and other groups who played The Cavern, were payed. There is a plaque commemorating the pub's links to the Beatles.

The most visited club in the street is of course the Cavern. Originally a jazz club it evolved into the most popular club for live bands, amongst whom were the Beatles who performed there from 1961-1963. The Cavern finally closed in 1973 and the warehouse was demolished. A second Cavern was built in the street, a convincing reconstruction using reclaimed bricks from the original club; it still draws the many Beatles fans from all over the world.

The Cavern Walks shopping mall now stands on the original site. Built between 1982-84 it was designed by Liverpool architect David Blackhouse. During the excavation work, five underground wells were discovered they had been originally excavated in 1850 for the purpose of providing water to the local population. The interior has a nine storey atrium and within are shops and offices. There is a statue of the Beatles inside the mall by John Doubleday and suspended over the stair way is piece of sculpture by Mike Badger, a Liverpool musician and artist. The terracotta relief work on the outside is by Cynthia Lennon, it shows doves and roses a reference to John's work for peace and his love of roses. The keystone in the archway over the Harrington Street car park entrance has a relief of a gorilla looking into a compact mirror as she applies lipstick. This is a humorous reply by David Blackhouse to the quote of British architect Norman Foster that "Art is to architecture like a lipstick to a gorilla", meaning that art is irrelevant.

John Lennon

A life size bronze statue of John Lennon by Dave Webster, stands
outside the Cavern, he is leaning against the brick wall, each brick
is inscribed with the names of all the groups and performers who
played at the Cavern. John Lennon's statue originally stood in a
doorway and showed him with a slicked back rocker hairstyle, as
he would have worn it during the early days prior to Brian Epstein's
management. Sadly the head was vandalised and David Webster
replaced the head giving John the floppy hairstyle that we see today.
The statue was also moved to the wall at the same time.

On a wall in Mathew Street, renamed Beatle Street is a sculpture by Liverpool artist Arthur Dooley. Entitled "Four Boys Who Shook The World." It shows the Madonna holding cherubs which represent the Beatles. When it was first erected fans stole the cherub of Paul, "Paul has taken wings and flown" gives the only explanation for his disappearance. A small cherub holding a guitar with the words "Lennon Lives" above it was added following his asssassination in 1980.

Nearby is a second wall of fame displaying the city's number one hits since 1952!

The musical theme is enhanced by a bench at the entrance to Mathew Street and two pairs of chairs in Button Street and Harrington Street. Made from wrought iron they have designs of musical instruments on them.

Three plaques on the side wall of Flanagan's Apple pub, of a painting, a poem and a liver bird with the inscription," Liverpool Dream", by Peter Corbett, Laurence Sidorczuk,Terence McGonigle and John Kelly.

Stanley Street

On a bench in Stanley Street sits the figure of a woman.Created by Fifties pop star Tommy Steele. Called "All the Lonely People" taking the line from the Lennon & McCartney song "Eleanor Rigby"

The old lady is resting on the bench, looking down at a tiny sparrow which sits beside her.

Inside the sculpture Tommy has left a four leaf clover for luck, a page from the Bible for our spiritual needs,a football sock recognising Liverpool's strong football following, Dandy and Beano comics representing comedy and four sonnets representing love.

The name Eleanor Rigby was spotted by Paul McCartney on a headstone in the church yard of St.Peter's Church Woolton, the place where he and John Lennon first met.

An electricity sub station which once powered the Cavern has been turned into a piece of art work, painted purple with flashing lights, best seen at night!

Waterfront

In 2004 Liverpool's waterfront became a World Heritage Site. The area includes The Pierhead, Stanley, Waterloo, and Wapping Docks, the Commercial District, parts of the Culture Quarter and the warehouses and Georgian houses along Duke Street.

Following its success in 2008 as the European Capital of Culture tourism is now a growth industry and Liverpool has much to offer as new museums and galleries open up.

Liverpool is once more a thriving city, rich with a diverse cultural heritage making it a city with many attractions to cater for many tastes.

To appreciate Liverpool's architecture along the waterfront it is best seen from the river. Three Graces, Liver Building,

Cunard Building and Port of Liverpool Building symbolise the Maritime aspect of the city. Further development in recent years has added to the landscape and the Liverpool Museum has already been given the title, the Fourth Grace. Viewed from the river the Anglican Cathedral towers over the city along with the Metropolitan Cathedral and the Radio City Tower.

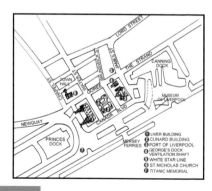

Albert Dock

Designed by Jesse Hartley and fellow civil engineer Philip Hardwick, Albert Dock was the first enclosed warehouse within the Liverpool Docks. It was the first structure in Britain to be built from brick, cast iron and stone thus making the warehouses fireproof. The dock complex was officially opened in April 1845 by Prince Albert. At the time the Albert Dock led the way in so far as ships cargoes could be loaded and unloaded directly from and to the warehouses, using the world's first hydraulic cranes.

(The Pump House Inn once housed the steam engines which supplied the high pressure water for the hydraulic hoists)

As the warehouses were bonded, which meant that import tax was payable only when the goods were ready to leave the warehouses and this also meant that the customs men did not have to be present when the cargoes arrived.

 At its height Albert Dock was trading with America, Africa and the Caribbean; its warehouses filled with supplies from these countries.

Despite the innovative design of Albert Dock by the 1860's the dock was losing business as the dock entrance was too narrow to admit the new larger steam ships. Trade fell away until Albert Dock was used as a cold store, producing ice for packing fish onboard the Liverpool's trawlers.

The Dock Road wall was also designed by Jesse Hartley, the stones that make up the wall came from the local quarry in Mount Street which is now St.James' cemetery. The supports of the demolished overhead railway can still be seen embedded in the walls at intervals along the Dock Road.

Running the length of the docks from north to south the overhead railway was also known as the Dockers Umbrella as it gave shelter from the rain. It was the world's first electrically operated overhead railway,opening in 1893 and still operating until 1956 when it was sadly demolished. Drinking fountains were inset at intervals along the wall, providing a welcoming drink for the dockers. One can be found at the

Salthouse Dock entrance which leads into Albert Docks.

Within the Albert Dock, and placed at the entrance to the Maritime Museum is an anchor from H.M.S. Conway, a ninety two gun battleship dating from 1839. It later became a training ship and was stationed on the Mersey.

Around the dock are several statues relating to Liverpool's past

boy at the back of the group is shown playing happily with a crab, unaware of his parents' anxiety of what may lie ahead for them.

Emigrants

A bronze statue by Mark de Graffenreid of an Irish Family commemorates the plight of many Irish families who were forced to leave Ireland during the potato famine which lasted from 1845-1852. During this time Ireland's population fell dramatically as many families set sail for Liverpool and for those who could afford the fare, America, all hoping to make a better life.

The sculpture shows the father looking out to sea as the small

Carter's Work Horse

Sculpted by Judy Boyt the work horse is a reminder of the important role these horses played, many transporting goods to and from the docks. At one time there were more than 20,000 horses working on the streets of Liverpool.

Billy Fury

Pre-dating the Beatles, Billy Fury was Liverpool's answer to Elvis Presley. Before he found fame as a singer Billy Fury worked as a deckhand on the "Formby" tugboat and he is fittingly placed looking out across the river.

The piece was created by Tom Murphy.

ate Gallery

So named after Sir Henry Tate of Tate and Lyle Sugar. Born in Chorley Lancashire in 1819, he was the son of a Unitarian Minister of the Dissenters Chapel. His family moved to Liverpool and at the age of thirteen Henry became apprentice in the grocery trade. After finishing his apprenticeship he bought his first business in Old Haymarket; by the time he had reached thirty five he had aquired five more grocers shops.

In 1859 Henry became a partner in the sugar refining company of John Wright and Co. eventually selling his grocery shops. On the death of John Wright the company changed its name to Henry Tate and Sons. In 1872 he bought the patent for making sugar cubes and this new innovation made him a milliionaire. In 1874 or thereabouts Henry Tate set up the Thames Refinery on the Thames in London and moved to London, setting up home in Park Hill Streatham.

In 1891 he was given the Freedom of the City of Liverpool and in 1898 finally accepted his Knighthood having turned it down earlier.

Henry Tate died one year later having given generous donations to several institutions. Amongst those which benefited were the University of Liverpool and the Royal Infirmary. He gave £500 towards books for the new library in Chorley and financed the building of libraries in Streatham, Brixton and Lambeth.

Apart from sugar his name is most closely associated with the arts as he founded the National Gallery of British Art, known as the Tate Britain, it opened in 1897 with works which he contributed from his private collection. Tate Modern, Tate St. Ives and the Tate Liverpool were to follow.

One of the most recognisable waterfronts in the world, the Liver Building, Port of Liverpool Building and Cunard Building, make up the Three Graces and dominate the waterfront. A fourth building, the new Museum of Liverpool has already been described as the Fourth Graces.

Running along the length of the Three Graces is Canada Boulevard which has a row of maple trees, Canada's national tree. Each pair of trees has a plaque set into the pavement bearing the names of the Canadian ships that were sunk during W.W.II The Canadian Navy was used to protect merchant plaque set into the pavement bearing the names of the ships as they came in and out of the port carrying vital supplies.

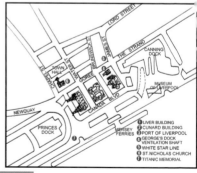

iver Building

The Liver building was built to house the Royal Liverpool Friendly Society Insurance Company.

Designed by Walter Aubrey Thomas and completed in 1911, this Grade One listed building was the first in Britain to be constructed using concrete blocks.

Taking pride of place on top of the domes perch two Liver birds, the symbol of Liverpool. Made from copper, the birds stand eighteen feet high and are held firmly in place because legend has that if the birds were to fly away, Liverpool would cease to exist. The birds also face in opposite directions, as they were designed to watch over the city (Our People) and out to sea (Our Prosperity.)

The birds were created by a German master carver, Carl Bernard Bartels who came to England on honeymoon in 1887 and decided to stay. He won a national competition to design the liver birds for the new building.

During World War 1 however, Bartels was interred on the Isle of Man and after the war was forcibly repatriated back to Germany, even though he had been a naturalised Briton for more than twenty years.

Such was the anti- German feeling at the time that his plans and blueprints were destroyed and any reference of him were removed from the records.

After many years of petitioning Carl Bernard Bartels work was recognised when the city posthumously awarded him with the "Citizen of Honour Award" at the time of the Liver Building's 100th Birthday, July 19th 2011.

The two clocks within the tower have a twenty five foot diameter and are larger than Big Ben in London. Chimes were installed in 1953 to commemorate those members of staff who lost their lives during the two world wars.

Port of Liverpool Building

Built as the head offices of the former Mersey Docks and Harbour Board. This Grade II listed building came about as a result of a competition with a prize of £300. The winning designers Sir Arnold Thornley and H.B. Hobbs in collaboration with Briggs and Wolstenholme. The style chosen is described as Edwardian Baroque and its central dome which was added to the design as the last minute is often compared to the dome of St.Paul's Cathedral in London. Construction started in 1904, the first nine months were spent in laying the foundations due to the close proximity to the river. To make sure that the basement would be water resistant the foundations were dug to a depth of 30-40' The building was completed in 1907 with a final cost of £250,000, with the internal design and furnishings adding a further £350,000. The grand stair case is lit by stained glass windows featuring maritme scenes and with references to those countries of what was once the British Empire.

The main entrance gates are decorated with shells, anchors and mermaids and with shields bearing the initials M.D. & B.H. The outside lighting is in the form of ships and Neptune holds the lights.Further reliefs of sailing ships can be seen around the exterior walls.

The main entrance doors have two female figures representing "Commerce" and "Industry" which were designed by Charles John Allen. On the floor of the main entrance is a mosaic showing the points of a compass. An impressive frieze around the reception area bears an inscription from Psalm 107:

*They that go down to the sea to
do business in great waters these
see the works of the lord and his
wonders of the deep Anno Domini
MCMVII"*

The building remained the head
offices until 1994 when the
company moved to Seaforth Dock.
The building was sold to Liverpool
based property company and after
plans were approved, work began
on major external and internal
restoration, being completed in 2009
at a cost of £10 million.

Cunard Building

The last of the Three Graces to be
built, construction started in 1914
and was completed in 1917 for
the Cunard Steamship Company.
Built on the site of the former
George's Dock part of the original
dock wall can still be seen within
the basement. Grade II listed
t was designed by W.E.Willink
and P.C.Thicknesse. The heavily
decorated building is in the style of
the Italian Renaissance and Greek
Revival. High up in the cornices of
the exterior are shields which bear
the names of the countries allies
during the First World War. Sculpted
heads of people from different
ethnic backgrounds are set above

the windows, illustrating the global
aspect of the city.

Besides it being the head
office of Cunard it was also the
gathering place for the Cunard
liner passengers prior to their
embarkation. The passengers
luggage was stored in the enormous
basement.The sub basement
was used as an air raid shelter
throughout the Second World War
and acted as the central A.R.P.
headquarters for the city.

Outside the building, facing the river,
is a bronze (now green) statue of a
man said to represent Victory. It is a
memorial to the employees who died
in the war; an inscription says:

"pro patria" ....."for ones' country"

Museum of Liverpool

At a cost of £72m the Museum of Liverpool is the latest addition to the waterfront. Designed by Danish architect Kim Neilsen and his company 3XN it is the first museum in the world to be dedicated solely to the history and culture of a city and also the largest to have been built in England for one hundred years.

As the site is a Unesco World Heritage site, concern was voiced as to the suitability of the new building, especially its close proximity to the Three Graces. It was feared the new building would detract and obstruct views of the historical waterfront landscape. The architect was very aware of this when he said "we had to be very respectful of that site, it is a World Heritage Site, actually a site where you should not have built maybe." Neilsen went on to say that he wanted to make a structure rather than a building and that it would be "more like a piece of land art ".

A steel frame construction, clad in patterned jura limestone, the museum's shape was inspired by origami, the Japanese art of paper folding. The museum is set over three floors with a stunning central spiral staircase connecting each gallery. Two large windows either end of the building measuring 8 metres high by 28 metres wide, open out onto views of the Pierhead and river.

Spanning the Leeds Liverpool canal it helps to connect the Pierhead and promenade to the Albert Dock.

aptain Johnny Walker

Merchant Sailors Memorial

This memorial lists the names of 1,390 men who lost their lives in the Second World War.The merchant navy suffered heavy losses as they fell victim to the U boats. Despite the heavy loss of life and ships, the merchant navy successfully brought in enough supplies to bring about an allied victory.

\mongst the many memorials on he waterfront there is one that is edicated to Captain John Walker.

iverpool was the headquarters of he North Atlantic Campaign during he Second World War.

:aptain Johnnie Walker was British Naval Officer and allied commander and hero of the Battle of the Atlantic, sinking more U boats than any other commander. Captain Walker was awarded DSO and three Bars R.N.

Designed by Tom Murphy.

Alfred Lewis Jones Memorial

This Grade II listed monument is of Alred Jones. Born in Wales, Alfred Jones began his career apprenticed to the African Steamship Company which was based in Liverpool. Eventually starting his own successful shipping business. With his growing business interests in West Africa he was described as the *"uncrowned King of West Africa."*

As a result of his many successful financial interests in West Africa Alfred Jones was able to give a generous donation to the Liverpool School of Tropical Medicine. He was instrumental in founding the school which today is one of the leading research schools making a major contribution into research and cures for tropical diseases.

The statue stands in front of the Liver Building facing the Mersey. On the top of the plinth is a female figure representing Liverpool, she is shown wearing a tunic with the Liverpool crest of the liver bird. In her left hand is a globe with a ship balancing on top; her right hand is extended in "welcoming commerce to the Port of Liverpool" At the base of the plaque there is a bronze profile and brief

description of Alfred Lewis Jones. On opposite sides of the base sit two more figures representing "The Fruits of Industry" and "Research".

Designed by Sir George Frampton

The Seven Seas

Made from forged steel and designed by Stanley English, this modern piece acts as a marker for the National Cycle Network. Set up by a charitable organisation Sustrans (Sustainable Transport) with help from the Lottery fund. The aim of the charity is to open up a network of cycle routes which will minimise the need to use major roads by using minor roads, canal towpaths, disused rail networks and pedestrian routes wherever possible.

George's Dock Ventilation Shaft

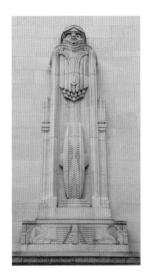

Georges Dock Ventilation Shaft was built in 1934 for the QueenswayTunnel. It is located on the Strand behind the Port of Liverpool Building. Designed by Herbert James Rowse in the Art Deco style he was influenced by the art and architecture of ancient Eygpt and the earlier discovery of the Tomb of Tuttankhamen.

The most interesting features are hidden from the main road. On the side of the building which faces the river is a seven foot high relief, a stylised figure of Mercury and depending on the time of day, the sun's shadows across the statue can give it quite a sinister appearance. Two black basalt figures sitting either side of the main entrance represent day and night. On the north and south sides are reliefs showing the various craftsmen who were involved in its construction, civil engineers, architects and designers.

On the east side of the building is a plaque in memory of the workmen who were killed during the construction of the Mersey Tunnel.

White star Line

On the corner of the Strand and James Street is the former headquarters of the shipping company. A distinctive building because of its red and white striped brick work,it was designed by Richard Norman Shaw. When news broke of the sinking of the Titanic people gathered here for news with the crowds stretching all the way to St. Nicholas Church.

Titanic Memorial

This granite monument was designed by William Goscombe John. Although the Titanic never came into the port of Liverpool due to its size, it was owned by the White Star Line, a Liverpool based company and was registered there. The owner of the White Star Line was Thomas Henry Ismay who bought the ailing shipping company in1867. He formed a partnership with Belfast shipbuilders Harland and Wolff whereby all of White Star Line ships would be built at the Belfast ship builders. In 1892 Ismay senior retired and his son Joseph Bruce Ismay took control of the company.The head office moved to the new building on the Strand at James Street. A distinctive red and white striped brick building work designed by Richard Norman Shaw.

Joseph Ismay wanted to build a ship to rival the liners of their competitor Cunard Line. The Titanic was built with the most up to date features and considered to be unsinkable.

The Titanic set sail on its maiden voyage from Southampton on 10th April 1912 bound for New York carrying some of the wealthiest people in the world as well as over one thousand emigrants from Ireland England and Europe hoping for a new life in America. Among the passengers were Joseph Ismay who normally accompanied his ships on their maiden voyage and Thomas Andrews, the head designer of the ship. Four days into the journey the ship struck an iceberg and within a matter of hours the ship sank. The Carpathia, ironically a ship from the rival Cunard Line was first to reach the Titanic. Of the 2,200 passengers and crew on board, only 700 survived. Although by law the ship had the required number of life boats, she did not have to carry any more life boats than a 10,000 ship even though she was equiped to carry up to 3,547 passengers and crew, she only had enough life boats for 962. In total there were only sixteen life boats and four collapsible boats which would have brought the capacity up to 1,178. Such was the belief that the ship was unsinkable many passengers refused to get into the life boats, when the order for women and children first was given, many women, not wanting to be separated from their husbands refused to climb into the boats and many were launched only partly filled. Among the passengers to survive was Joseph Bruce Ismay who after helping with the evacuation managed to get into one of the last boats, collapsible boat C.Thomas Andrews realizing that were not enough lifeboats stood back; he was one of the passengers who perished in the disaster along with the captain, Captain Edward John Smith.

The ship's orchestra, led by their conductor William Hartley, remained behind to play with the hope of calming the trapped passengers. None of the musicians survived. The sound of a lone violinist was heard playing "Nearer My God To Thee" as the ship disappeared.

There is a plaque in the foyer of the Philharmonic Hall honouring their bravery as J.F.Clarke, a viola player in the orchestra and native Liverpudlian was one of the musicians who lost his life. An inscription on the plaque states:

"courage and compassion joined to make the hero and the man complete."

The Titanic memorial at the Pierhead is dedicated to the loss of the two hundred and forty four men who remained in the engine room to keep the ship supplied with power, thus enabling it to remain afloat for as long as possible and therefore enabling many passengers to escape.

t was pointed out to me by a retired docker, that the figures of the stokers are not accurate in so far as they are wearing their belts with the buckles at the front whereas stokers always turned the buckles towards their backs because the heat from the furnaces would have made the buckles so hot that the stokers skin would have burned. He also remarked that the sculptor may not have been very pleased to have had that pointed out to him after its completion!

St. Nicholas Church

Facing the Titanic memorial is the church of Our Lady and St.Nicholas; A Grade II listed building it is better known as St Nicholas or St. Nicks, the sailors church,St.Nicholas being the patron saint of sailors.

There has been a church on this site since the thirteenth century. Over time the church was enlarged and eventually the main body was rebuilt. The River Mersey used to reach the walls of the church yard at high tide until George's dock was built in 1767.

Disaster struck one Sunday morning in 1810 when the old steeple collapsed crashing to the ground and killing twenty eight of the congregation. The tower was quickly rebuilt and completed in 1815.

Air raids during the Second World War completely destroyed the church. Work started in 1949 to rebuild St. Nicholas Church and it was eventually re-consecrated in 1952. Its distinctive lantern tower with a gilded copper weather vane of a ship is a familiar landmark for those sailing into Liverpool.

In the interior there are two chapels either side of the main altar. St. Peter's to the left is dedicated to the old parish church of St. Peter's which stood on Church Street. (A gold cross marks the spot in Church Street.) The wooden table in the chapel was once the altar of the old church and the large wooden cross is made from its charred timbers. St.Mary's Chapel has a bronze statue of Mary standing in the prow of a boat, the work of Liverpool sculptor Arthur Dooley. A book of rememberance to the sailors who were lost at sea is on display in the chapel.

In the church gardens there is a tribute to the people of Liverpool who lost their lives during the blitz as Liverpool was the nerve centre of the Battle of the Atlantic it suffered heavy bombing raids. The statue shows a small boy playing with a toy plane, stretching up into the sky while his mother, clutching a baby, is desperately trying to reach him in order to take them to shelter from an oncoming air raid. Designed by Tom Murphy I think it is one of the most moving pieces as it really brings home how much suffering the people endured during that time.

In Chapel Street, set into the perimeter wall of the church is a drinking fountain dating from 1885. It is in memory of William Shaw Simpson,a local businessman who did much to raise funds for many charities, particularly the Irish Distress Fund.

Within the grounds of St. Nicholas Church is the Sarpedon Bell, it is there as a reminder of the church's association with sailors. The bell came from the Blue Funnel Line owned ship, the Sarpedon. All of the Blue Funnel Line ships were given names taken from Greek mythology and history.

Mersey Chambers

Sitting behind the church gardens is the Grade II listed Mersey Chambers Building.It was built in 1878 for the shipping company, Harrison Shipping Line. Overlooking St. Nicholas Churchyard, Mersey Chambers was designed by G.E. Grayson, a Liverpool architect. The public gardens were laid out in 1891 in memory of James Harrison who was a partner in the shipping company. Looking down from the roof of the building is the third Liver Bird, half the size of its neighbours who are perched on top of the Liver Building.

Princes Landing Stage

Further along the river heading north,are the remains of the original landing stage of Princes Dock. Emigrants set sail for America from this point, hoping for a better life. Sadly this important landmark has been badly neglected and is in danger of falling into the Mersey. Ironically a short distance from this is the new Princes landing stage built for the enormous liners bringing people into the city, some perhaps the great grandchildren of those emigrants, who may be coming to search of their roots.

Waterloo Warehouse

Grade II listed, Waterloo warehouse is built within the Waterloo Docks and named after Wellington's victory at the Battle of Waterloo. The docks were opened in 1834 as world trade grew. In 1844 an observatory was built on the dock wall for astronomical and meteorological observations, providing accurate times for ships chronometers which were essential for safe navigation. The observatory was moved to Bidston Hill on the Wirral Peninsula in 1868.

After the repeal of the Corn Laws in 1846 trade in grain grew and with that demand for storage. The dock was split into two and huge grain warehouses built around them. Designed by George Fosbery Lyster engineer in chief of the Mersey Docks and Harbour Board who had taken over from Jesse Hartley. The warehouses opened in 1868, originally there were three blocks but only the east block remains. The docks closed for shipping in 1988 and Waterloo Warehouse was converted into luxury apartments in 1990.

In 1962 the artist L.S.Lowry visited Liverpool and made an oil painting of Waterloo Docks, showing the warehouse. The painting is presently on loan to the Walker Art Gallery.

Stanley Dock Conservation Area

North of the Pierhead is the Stanley Dock conservation area which takes in the dock boundary wall, part of the Leeds Liverpool Canal and their locks, Stanley, Collingwood and Salisbury Docks, The Victoria Tower and the surrounding warehouses. All these structures have played an important part in the maritime and trading history of Liverpool.

Nowadays the sheer size of the warehouses makes any new development a huge challenge. Plans to re-develop will also have certain conditions attached to accomodate its present tenants, pipistrelle bats. Speciallly constructed tubes are to be installed to allow access to the four lift shafts in which they currently live.

Thankfully this once neglected area is now part of a multi million pound regeneration programme which will hopefully bring life back into this once bustling part of Liverpool.

North and South Stanley Dock Warehouses

Built by Jesse Hartley, Stanley Dock was opened in 1848. The massive warehouse was used to store imported goods,one warehouse being built solely for the storage of tobacco.

Tobacco Warehouse

This warehouse was designed by A.G.Lyster who had succeeded his father, George Lyster as engineer in chief to the Mersey Docks and Harbour Board. The largest brick built warehouse in the world it takes up thirty two acres. Standing fourteen stories high with forty two bays divided by seven loading bays. The warehouse closed in the eighties as the docks fell victim to a down turn in trade. The ground floor now houses the Sunday Heritage Market. The only sign of its former use is a raised inscription high above on the wall of the Dock Road side of the warehouse saying "MDE, 1900" and "Tobacco Warehouse."

Victoria Tower

The Victoria Tower, known locally as the Docker's clock, it was built in 1848 and designed by Jesse Hartley. The tower houses six clocks so that the ships could set the correct time as they sailed out to sea.

There is also a bell tower whose bell would ring out to warn of any high tides or fog.

Street Names

Abercromby Square
Named after General Sir Ralph Abercromby commander of the British Army in Eygpt who was killed at the Battle Alexandria in 1801.

Argyle Street
Named after John Campbell, Duke of Argyle

Basnett Street
Laid out between 1770-1780 by the Basnett family in memory of Chrisopher Basnett who was the first minister of Key Street Chapel, the meeting place of the Protestant Dissenters. Key Street was later demolished to make way for Exchange Station.

Berry Street
Named after Henry Berry, the city's second dock engineer, responsible for Salthouse, King's and George's Docks, he lived in a house at the junction with Duke Street.

Blackburne Place
Named after John Blackburne, a salt refiner and supporter of the slave trade.He became Mayor of Liverpool in 1760. Having bought a plot of land he built Blackburne House where he lived between 1785-1790.

Bold Street
Named after Jonas Bold who held the lease for the land during the 18th century. Slave trader, sugar merchant and banker.He became Mayor of Liverpool in 1802

Button Street
Laid out in 1722 it was named after John Button, the leaseholder of the land.

Campbell Street
Named after George Campbell,slave trader and sugar merchant. He was Mayor of Liverpool in 1763.

Canning Place
Situated on the site of the old Canning Dock, named after George Canning M.P. and P.M., he gave his support to the campaign for the abolition of slavery.

Cases Street
Named after Thomas Case, brother-in-law to Sarah Clayton.

Castle Street
One of the original streets, named after Liverpool Castle which was erected in the 13th century.

Catherine Street
Named after Catherine Jones whose property developer son, William Jones was the first to build a house on the street.

Chapel street
One of the original streets, it was named after the Chapel of St. Mary Del Quay the site of which now stands St. Nicholas Chuch.

Church Street
After St. Peter's Church, built in 1704 it was the first church to be built following the Reformation; it was demolished as late as 1919.

Clarence Street
Named after the Duke of Clarence, later William IV. He visited Liverpool in 1790 when Clarence Street was laid. The Prince was very popular in Liverpool as he spoke in the House of Lords in support of the slave trade. He was given Freedom of the Borough.

Clayton Square
Sarah Clayton, who laid out the square and the neighbouring streets which she named after her mother's maiden name and her married sisters surnames, between 1745 and 1750; she was the daughter of William Clayton M.P.

Colquitt Street
John Colquitt was Collector of Customs, his home was in Hanover Street.

Concert Street
In 1840 a concert hall was built on the corner of the street to replace an earlier one which had been destroyed in a fire.

Copperas Hill
Named after a copper works which once operated on that site. Forced to move in 1756 because of the noxious smell.

Crosshall Street
Named after the family home of the Crosse family who had an influential role in the development of Liverpool.

Dale Street
One of the original streets, it led to the dale through which a stream flowed from Moss Lake to the Pool of Liverpool.

Derby Square
Named after Lord Derby who obtained a grant for the

development of a market square on the site of Liverpool Castle.

Duke Street
After the Duke of Cumberland, brother of King George II. It was originally the road to the quarry, when the quarry was exhausted St. James Cemetery was built on the site.

Elliot Street
After Sir George Augustus Elliot, who defended Gibraltar between 1779 and 1783.

Falkner Square
Laid out by Edward Falkner, he intended to name it Wellington Square but it was named "Falkner's Folly" at the time as it was considered to be too far out of town.

Gambier Terrace
Named after Admiral James Gambier (1756-1833),commander of the British fleet at the Battle of Copenhagen (1807)

Goree
An island off the coast of Cape Verde were slaves were held prior to being shipped to the plantations.

Hanover Street
Originally called King Street it was renamed after the reigning family of the time.

Hardman Street
Named after Mrs. Hardman, the widow of John Hardman of Allerton, M.P.for Liverpool in 1754,who owned the land through which the street ran.

Hope Street
William Hope, built his house in the street, on the corner of Hardman Street, the site now occupied by the Philharmonic Hall.

Huskisson Street
Commemorates William Huskisson M.P. who was killed at the opening of the Liverpool Manchester Railway in1830.

James Street
Originally named St.James Street it was changed to James Street in the seventeenth century.

Kent Street
Named after Richard Kent, merchant and ship-owner, in 1768 he had a house built on the corner of Kent Street and Duke Street, the first house to be built on that street.

Knight Street
Named after brothers John and James Knight who laid out the street in 1785.

Leece Street
Named after William Leece merchant and ship owner, who lived in Water Street.

Lime Street
Originally Limekiln Lane,in the eighteenth century there were lime kilns where Lime Street Station now stands.

Lord Street
Originally Molneux or Lord Molyneux Street, after Viscount Molyneux, who also held the lease to Liverpool Castle.A supporter of James II during the Glorious Revolution of 1688.

London Road
So named as it was the main road out of Liverpool to London

Lydia Ann Street
Named after the wife of George Perry, manager of the Phoenix Foundry to which the street led.

Maryland Street
Named by Mr.Hunter, a Virginia tobacco merchant who lived in Mount Pleasant it recognises the importance to Liverpool of the slave produced tobacco plantations in Maryland.

Moorfields
Originally MoorCroft. Part of the Moore family estate it was first mentioned in the public records of 1697.

Mount Street
A street that led to the Mount Zion pleasure gardens. It was on this site that the Anglican Cathedral was built.

North John Street
Formerly Saint John Street it took its name from lands that belonged to the chantry of Saint John in the Church of Our Lady and Saint Nicholas.

Old Hall Street
Formerly White Acres or Peppard Street. The mansion house and seat of the Moores was originally called Moore Hall. When the family moved to Bank Hall the former home was referred to as the "Old Hall" and

so the street leading to it became known as Old Hall Street.

Parliament Street
Originally Townsend Lane it was renamed after the Act of Parliament of 1773, it marked the boundary between Liverpool and Toxteth Park.

Paradise Street
Originally Common Shore. The engineer Thomas Shore, who built the first Liverpool Dock owned land on Common Shore. When the street was laid out he named it Paradise Street after the street of that name in Rotherhithe, London, where he once lived.

Parr Street
Named after Thomas Parr, wealthy slave trader and banker who built his house in Colquitt Street. He boasted that he had the "handsomest house, wife and horse in Liverpool."

Pilgrim Street
Originally Jamieson Street it was renamed after a privateer called the "Pilgrim" She brought into Barbados a prize, which along with its cargo sold for the enormous sum of £190,000.

Ranelagh Street
The Ranelagh Tea Gardens stood on the site which is now occupied by the Adelphi Hotel.

Renshaw Street
Brothers John and Edward Renshaw owned a ropery on this site.

Rodney Street
Named after Admiral Lord George Rodney in recognition of the part he played in the victory over the French fleet off St. Lucia in the West Indies(1782) during the American War of Independence.

Roscoe Street
Named after Liverpool's "greatest son." A merchant, philanthropist and passionate abolitionist. His father was a market gardener and owned a public house in Mount Pleasant, from which Roscoe Street runs.

Seel Street
Named after Thomas Seel,slave trading merchant and property owner, his house was on Hanover Street with extensive gardens through which the street was laid out.

Shaw Street
The street was laid out by John Shaw a Liverpool councillor whose father through marriage had inherited the large Everton estate of the Halsall family. The first house on the street was built in 1829.

Sir Thomas Street
Originally Sir Thomas Buildings, it commemorates Sir Thomas Johnson, Mayor of Liverpool in 1715. and Member of Parliament.He was left a fortune by his father, he traded as a merchant in sugar and tobacco but in 1723 he lost in speculation his and his father's fortune and died in poverty in London in 1728.

Slater Street
Named after Gill Slater, first captain of the Liverpool Volunteers raised in 1766 when a French invasion was threatened.

Stanley Street
Originally New Street it was laid out in1740 through land that belonged to the Derby family from the Moores of Bank Hall.

Tarleton Street
Named after John Tarleton, the father of a slave trading family in Liverpool. Three of Tarleton's sons were involved in the slave trade between 1786-1788, owning shares in as many as fifty two ships. The fourth son, Banastre became M.P. and a strong anti- abolitionist.

Tithebarn Street
Originally Moor Street, Lord Molyneux, Lord of the Manor built his tithe barn in Moor Street in 1514.

Victoria Street
Named after Queen Victoria, it was laid out in the 1860's as a new approach to Lime Street Station and St.George's Hall.

Water Street
Originally called Bonke or Bank Street it was one of the seven original streets to be laid out,so named as it led down to the river bank.

William Brown Street
Once called Shaw's Brow it was renamed William Brown Street in recognition of his contribution to Liverpool, giving the city its library and museum.

Index of Architects and Sculptors

Charles John Allen (1863-1956)
Panels St.George's Hall

Figures on Queen Victoria Monument

Statues outside Port of Liverpool Building

Carl Bernard Bartels (1866-1955)
Liver Bird

Stephen Broadbent (1961-)
Reconciliation

Sheppard and Warlock bronzes

Thomas Brock (1847-1922)
Gladstone Statue

W.D.Caroe (1857-1938)
Adelphi Bank

Siegfried Charoux (1896-1967)
The Family (flanking Newsroom War Memorial)

Sir Charles Cockerell (1788-1863)
Liverpool Branch of the Bank of England

Interior of St. Georges Hall

Arthur Dooley (1929-1944)
Beatles, Four Boys Who Shook the World
Madonna St. Nicholas Church

John Foster (1876-1846)
Huskisson Mausoleum
Oratory
St.Andrews Church

Sir George Frampton (1860-1928)
The following statues in St.John's Gardens:

William Rathbone

Sir Arthur Forwood

Thomas Major Lester

Sir Frederick Gibberd (1908-1984)
Metropolitan Cathedral.

G.E.Grayson (1833-1912)

British Foreign Marine Insurance Company

Mersey Chambers

Jesse Hartley (1780-1860)
Albert Dock and warehouses

Stanley Dock North and South Warehouses

Dock Wall

Victoria Tower

William Goscombe John (1860-1952)
Titanic Memorial

Thomas Harrison (1744-1829)

The Lyceum

William Goscombe John (1860-1952)

Drummer Boy St.John's Gardens

Titanic Memorial

Albert Bruce Joy (1842-1924)

Alexander Balfour

George Fosbery Lyster (1821-1899)

Waterloo Warehouse

A.G.Lyster (1852-1920)

Gladstone Graving Dock

Tom Murphy (1949-)
Chavasse Memorial
Sir John and Cecil Moores
Billy Fury
Captain John Walker
Liverpool Blitz

Sir James Picton (1805-1889)

Corn Exchange

Hargreaves Building

Herbert Rowse (1887-1963)

St.George's Ventilation Shaft

Martins Bank

Philharmonic Hall

India Building

Giles Gilbert Scott (1880-1960)

Anglican Cathedral

Richard Norman Shaw (1831-1912)

Albion House (White Star Line Building.)

F.M.Simpson

Victoria Memorial

Walter Aubrey Thomas (1859-1934)

Royal Liver Building

Tower Building

Walter Thomas

Philharmonic Dining Rooms

The Vines

P.C.Thicknesse. (Willink and Thicknesse)

Cunard Building

Liverpool College of Art Extension

Dave Webster (1946-)

John Lennon Mathew Street

Beatles Hard day's Night Hotel

Sir Richard Westmacott (1775-1856)

Nelson Memorial

W.E.Willink (1856-1924) (Willink and Thicknesse)

Cunard Building

Liverpool College of Art Extension

John Wood (1704-1754)

Liverpool Town Hall

James Wyatt (1746-1813)

Liverpool Town Hall (rear extension and interior)

First United States consul anywhere in the world James Murray, appointed in 1790

Stanley Dock, world's largest brick built building.

Elgar's Pomp and Circumstance March No 1 was dedicated to Liverpool by the composer, had its premier October 1901.

Battle of the Atlantic planned, fought and won from Liverpool.

Railways, municipal trams, electric trains, and the helicopter all pioneered in Liverpool. Liverpool and Manchester first cities to have intercity rail link

The University of Liverpool (Victoria Building) was the original Red Brick University.

First school for the blind

First school for deaf children.

First High school for girls, Blackburne House

Juvenile court

R.S.P.C.A

N.S.P.C.C.

First life boat station

Public baths and wash house founded by Kitty Wilkinson.

Council house

Medical officer for health

District nurse

Purpose built ambulance

Polarising x ray at the Southern Hospital.

Richard Caton, a pyhsician practising in Liverpool, published his discovery of brain waves in 1875

Modern day anaesthetics pioneered by Thomas Cecil Gray.

School of tropical medicine cure for malaria

Radio tuning

First Nobel prize winner 1902 Robert Ross

First lending library

Athenaeum society

Public art conservation centre.

First British public Art Gallery, Walker Art Gallery.

Home to the first chess club Liverpool Chess Club.

The oldest rugby club, Liverpool Rugby Club

Inventor of the Crossword, Liverpool born, Arthur Wynne

Inventor of Meccano constuction toys, Liverpool born Frank Hornby.

First mosque in England established by William Abdullah Quilliam.

Notes

Notes

Notes

Notes

Notes

Notes